A STEP-BY-STEP GUIDE WITH TAILORED, PRACTICAL, AND EASY-TO-FOLLOW STRATEGIES FOR ACHIEVING FINANCIAL PEACE AND LASTING PROSPERITY

THE BLACK WOMAN'S *Guide To* BUILDING WEALTH

JOYCE IBITOYE

Contents

Introduction

January 28th arrived. It was finally payday. A day that should have brought relief, but instead, it brought anxiety. The bills were stacked high on my living room floor, each a reminder of my growing financial struggles. I already knew my entire salary wouldn't be enough to cover even half of these bills.

I prioritised paying rent—as I did not fancy living on the street mid-winter. After topping up the electricity and gas meters and paying a few more bills, there was barely anything left for food. I was already worrying about how I'd stretch what little we had until the next payday, a whole month away.

Just then, the doorbell rang. My heart sank as I peeked through the curtains. It was Mr Bailey, the council's collections officer. Panic set in. I quickly turned off the living room light, hoping he'd leave if he thought no one was home. But he wasn't easily deterred.

"Miss Ibitoye, I know ye're in. You cannae hide forever," his voice echoed through the door.

My dear girls couldn't understand why we were huddled in the back room with the lights off. I whispered that we were playing a game of hide-and-seek, but as I looked into my eldest daughter's eyes, I knew she saw right through my lie. She understood more than I wished she did.

That day was a turning point. I realised I couldn't keep living in fear—fear of the postman, fear of unpaid bills, fear of not being able to provide for my children. Something had to change. I needed to take control of my finances, not just for me but also for my girls.

I started where many do: personal finance books. They offered great advice on budgeting, saving, and setting financial goals, but they missed something crucial—they didn't speak to the unique challenges Black women face. They didn't address the pay disparities, the job insecurities, or the cultural responsibilities that weigh heavily on our financial decisions.

Jobs that pay well are hard to find for us. And even when we do, we're constantly having to prove ourselves. Job security is uncertain for everyone nowadays, but it's worse for us. When companies downsize, guess who's usually the first to go? That's right: Black women. We are often laid off first, without fair compensation, or we have to fight tooth and nail for what others take for granted (Cox, 2023).

As Black women, our challenges extend far beyond the workplace. We are often the backbone of our families and communities, carrying financial and emotional burdens. Many of us are single-handedly raising our families, with 86% of Black single-parent households headed by Black women (Office for National Statistics, 2023). Covering all the bills on modest incomes puts us at a significant financial disadvantage—even the best money management skills can only stretch so far.

Then there's the issue of the "Black tax." If you're not familiar with it, let me explain. The Black tax refers to the financial support many of us provide our struggling extended families. This challenge is widespread among first, second, or third-generation immigrants. Being an immigrant is tough enough—you're in a new and unfamiliar environment, often starting from scratch in a low-paid job or perhaps juggling work with studies. On top of that, you have family members back home relying on you for financial support.

It's a heavy burden, yet surprisingly, the Black tax is rarely discussed in finance books. How do we support our families without jeopardising our own financial future? Understanding the impact of the Black tax is so important that I've dedicated an entire chapter to this crucial topic.

I often wonder why financial victories seem so elusive, even after we invest in education, work tirelessly, and show unwavering dedication. The truth is we operate within an economic system that wasn't designed with our success in mind. Not landing that dream job? It's not because you're lazy. Struggling to get that promotion or raise? It's not due to a lack of initiative or intelligence. Facing endless performance reviews? It's not because you're the "angry Black woman."

Recognise your resilience, for it's not just a personal journey but a collective battle against a system that needs rewriting.

Let me paint you a data-backed picture so you know I am not just making this stuff up:

While the average household wealth in the UK is around £286,000 (Office for National Statistics, 2021), the average wealth for Black households is only £34,000 (Office for National Statistics, 2020). That's a staggering difference. Wouldn't you like to know why such a vast gap exists and how you can rise above the average?

Who do you think bears the brunt of this inequality? You've guessed it! Black women. The gender pay gap means women often earn less than men, but for Black women, race and gender combine to make the gap even wider. I searched for a Black female CEO of a publicly traded company in the UK and found none. The only Black women CEOs I found were those who built their companies from the ground up. According to WOB Directors (n.d.):

- There are still no Black women on the boards of FTSE 100 companies.
- Over half of Black women in senior leadership roles have resigned due to racial bias in the workplace.
- Forty-four per cent of Black women believe they don't receive the same professional development opportunities as their non-Black female colleagues.
- Black women are also the least likely to be among the UK's top earners (London School of Economics and Political Science, 2021).

As I could not find comprehensive financial help that addressed my unique financial woes, I began a journey of learning and unlearning, adapting the advice I found to fit my reality. This book is the result of that journey. It's not just a guide to managing money; it's a roadmap for overcoming the specific financial challenges that Black women face. It's about empowering you to take control of your financial story, just as I did on that cold January day. And yes, I will share how my story with Mr Bailey unfolded as we go on, but more importantly, I will show you how you can transform your financial situation.

This book is for the woman striving for financial security and freedom, even when the odds are stacked against her. Financial abundance is within reach, and I want to see you thrive, armed with the tools and knowledge to navigate financial systems and build wealth for yourself, your family, and future generations.

We'll cover everything from budgeting and managing debt to savvy saving strategies. And it's not just about the "how" but also the "why"—why we make our financial choices. Understanding this leads to better money management and lasting prosperity.

Finance isn't just something I dabble in—it's my life's work. I've spent years studying it, becoming a chartered accountant, and working for over 25 years in the finance industry. My focus? Personal and corporate finance: tackling money matters head-on. I've seen the damage caused by not understanding financial basics, and now I'm here to raise the alarm. You'll also find snippets of my own financial journey throughout these pages.

I've led workshops on financial freedom and offered one-on-one coaching. My "before-and-after" financial transformations give me confidence. The tips I share are the same ones that turned my finances around. I hope they'll do the same for you.

I highly recommend reading this book from start to finish. At the conclusion of each chapter, you'll discover a summary of core lessons and exercises designed to help you apply what you've learned right away.

Now, as promised, let me share how my game of cat and mouse with Mr Bailey finally played out.

I was fortunate, though it didn't feel that way at the time. Mr Bailey, posing as the postman, gained entry to my flat, catching me off guard. The fear of losing my few possessions overwhelmed me. I must have appeared a mess, with messy hair and tear-streaked mascara-covered cheeks. Fortunately, Mr Bailey proved much kinder than the fearsome monster I had imagined. Sensing my distress, he swiftly took action to ease the situation, even going as far as making me a comforting cup of tea in my kitchen. Engaging in a game of peekaboo with my daughters, he helped restore a sense of calm to us all.

"Right then, lassie," he said, "how've ye landed yerself in this wee bit of a pickle?" His voice was kind. I explained my struggles: not earning enough, part-time work, blah blah, blah!

He asked to use my phone (before the era of mobile phones), called the council, and negotiated a settlement figure on my behalf. I only had to pay a fraction of the bill. Problem solved!

This was my lucky day—and, no, it wasn't because I got most of my bill cancelled, but because I was forced to confront a situation I had been dodging for months. All that suffering and anxiety came to an end. If Mr Bailey had not forced himself into my apartment, I would have continued to live in fear, and the problem would only have gotten worse. And, yes, Mr Bailey forcing his way is not cool. I totally agree. There are laws against that kind of behaviour now, but first, this was the wild wild west of the 90s, and second, I am choosing to focus only on the outcome—a problem that had terrorised me for months was finally over. As Mr Bailey rightly said, **the lesson here is that we can't hide from money problems.** Ignoring them makes things worse and messes with our health. We must confront our money issues head-on, even when they seem impossible. I have found that things are never as bad as our mind leads us to believe.

Are you tired of feeling overwhelmed by your finances? It's time to take control and make a change. With the right conversation, helpful books such as this one, practical exercises, and intentional actions, you can transform your financial situation and achieve true peace of mind. Let this book be your guide on this journey towards financial freedom. Don't let fear hold you back any longer; this stuff really works!

Let me share a quick success story to show you what's possible. One of my coaching clients was drowning in debt and struggling to make ends meet, much like I once was. Following the strategies outlined in this book, she cleared her debts and bought her dream home. Now, she's on the verge of buying a second property to generate extra income. Her journey proves that financial success is within reach for all of us.

Remember, money is a tool—not something to be idolised. When used wisely, it serves your dreams, allowing you to focus on what truly matters: spirituality, family, health, and community. This book is about making money work for you, enriching your life rather than controlling it.

Chapter One

EMBRACING OUR FINANCIAL REALITIES

In the vibrant village of Ubeji, there lived twin siblings Akello and Zuri. This small fishing village got by solely on fishing, and everyone was involved in the fish business, including the siblings' mum and dad. As with most locals, Akello and Zuri's lives were filled with the harsh realities of poverty. The education facilities were poor, and jobs were a distant dream.

Akello, older by a mere five minutes, was the dreamer. He often wished for a better life but felt shackled by his circumstances. "Why was I born poor?" he'd lament, blaming everything from luck to his ancestors for his woes. He did not do well with his education either. "What's the point?" he often asked.

However, Zuri, the more adventurous sibling, had a different outlook on life. Sure, she'd grumble about the lack of opportunities, but her complaints were always followed by a positive outlook. "Life's not fair, but maybe there's a secret stash of opportunities hidden somewhere."

The adventurous Zuri faced more challenges due to being the younger sister in a place that favoured educating boys. Despite all these challenges, Zuri was determined not to let poverty and lack of opportunities shape her future. She took advantage of every opportunity before her. She excelled in school, burning the midnight oil for that extra edge.

One sunny afternoon, a rare opportunity appeared in Ubeji in the form of a talent show for the young people of Akello and Zuri's age. The grand prize was a scholarship to a prestigious school in the bustling capital city.

Akello scoffed, "What's the point? We're just villagers with no influence."

But Zuri's eyes sparkled with excitement. "Who says we can't dazzle them with our village rhythm?" she teased, nudging Akello.

But Zuri didn't care that her brother was sceptical; she went all in. She rallied the village youngsters, and they practised their unique drumming skills and choreographed a show that wowed even the moon.

When the day of the talent show arrived, Akello refused to participate. Zuri led the show with infectious enthusiasm. Their performance was a booming success. The results? Zuri and two other youngsters won the scholarship! Akello was wide-eyed and astonished. "I thought nothing could change," he murmured, shaking his head in disbelief.

Zuri grinned, holding the scholarship letter. "Change isn't just necessary; it's an adventure waiting to happen!" she exclaimed, hugging her bewildered brother.

Our three prize winners went off for an education in the capital, labouring long and hard for three years. When they returned, magic unfolded. They shared their skills, sparking new businesses and even a fishery college. Ubeji transformed into a beacon of hope and wealth.

And so, with laughter echoing through Ubeji, their newfound prosperity, wealth, and freedom, everybody lived happily ever after. Everyone except Akello.

Akello's views of life did not change much despite his sister's good fortune. He was still his old self. By the time Zuri returned, Akello was working full-time with his long-suffering dad, having flunked school with no other means of earning. He never stopped complaining. He was deeply resentful that Zuri had all the "lucky breaks." He attributed her luck to being a woman. "Women get all the breaks," he lamented. *"What about me? When will my lucky break come?"*

You've probably figured out the lessons from this story by now. We're like Akemi and Zuri on different days, living in a world where not everyone gets a silver spoon. I totally get Akello's sadness. Who wouldn't want a better life, especially in this hyper-connected world? We see how others live, and it's hard not to envy their lifestyles. All humans are equal and have value, but let's face it: we don't all get the same chances. But like Zuri, facing our realities head-on and refusing to be defeated is crucial for progress.

I had this real eye-opener during a lunch chat with a friend. I poured my heart out about money problems and boom! He put a stop to it. "Please, Joyce, not again. I'm tired and bored of hearing about your debts year after year; instead of moaning, fix it."

His words stung, and I sulked all the way home, thinking, *"What does he know about my life?"*

But then, I realised something. My friend is kind and loving and wants the best for me. His words stung me, but they had a lot of truth. He was right; every chat we'd had in the last year had been about my money worries.

I didn't realise it at the time, but I was actually going through the stages of grief that many of us feel when life doesn't unfold as we hoped. I had always pictured a different kind of life for myself. I never planned to be a single mother. I assumed that landing a well-paid job would be straightforward, which would naturally make taking care of my family much easier.

Much like Akello, I hadn't fully faced the truth about my financial situation. I felt sad, angry, and a bit silly for borrowing money for further education, even though my goal was to get a better job. Like Akello, I found myself asking, 'Why me?' I was scared and didn't know where to start with my money problems.

LISTING: A TOOL FOR EMPOWERMENT

One way to calm this financial storm is surprisingly simple yet incredibly effective: I wrote down all my money worries. By listing my money problems, I took a critical step toward managing my anxiety and finding solutions. The act of putting my worries into words brought a sense of relief. It was as if I were taking back control over my financial situation.
Imagine your problems as buzzing flies constantly circling around your head. Now imagine writing each of those problems down. Every issue you write down is like catching one of those flies and putting it in a jar. They're still there but no longer buzzing around your head. They're contained, quieter, and suddenly seem more manageable.

This act of writing does a few essential things for us. First, it helps us acknowledge what's bothering us. Acknowledgement is the first step toward acceptance. You can't address what you don't acknowledge. This simple recognition can be transformative, opening up a path toward finding solutions and feeling hopeful about your financial future.

Moreover, when our problems are clearly laid out in front of us, we can start to organise them. Which issue requires immediate attention? Which one can wait? What steps can we take to start addressing each one? This process not only organises our problems but also empowers us, making the possible solutions less daunting. You might even find yourself thinking, "Is that all?" I thought my problems were worse.

The act of writing down your money problems is not just a simple exercise; it's an act of self-care and empowerment. It's transitioning from a state of passivity and worry to active problem-solving, a step toward reclaiming financial control. Remember! Even if our money problems aren't our fault, it's still up to us to sort them out.

Feeling overwhelmed by money worries? Grab a pen and paper. It could be the key to clearing your mind and tackling those issues step-by-step.

Finally, be mindful that solutions won't happen overnight; it's a journey. The main aim here is to find peace and clarity in the present moment. Every step forward, no matter how small, is progress. So, let's face our financial hurdles with determination, knowing we possess the strength and capability to transform our financial landscape. Together, we can rewrite our money narrative and pave the way for a brighter, more empowered future.

CHAPTER ONE—CORE LESSONS

- **Attitude Shapes Results:** Two people facing similar challenges can have different outcomes. A positive attitude brings success, while negativity holds us back.
- **Strive for Excellence:** Give your best effort in what matters. Zuri excelled in school, opening doors for her. Commit to finishing this book and its exercises for financial breakthrough.

- **Taking Charge:** Own your current financial situation and seek solutions instead of dwelling on problems.
- **Seek Support and Wisdom:** Supportive friends or mentors offering valuable advice can spark personal growth, even if it's tough to hear.
- **Believe in Yourself:** Trust in your ability to make changes. Your determination is critical to improving your finances.

Chapter One—Exercise

Start With a Simple List

- Write down every money problem, big or small.
- Use pen and paper or create a digital list—whatever works best for you.
- Keep adding to your list as you remember other issues.

Enjoy the Process

- Get creative, and make the process enjoyable.
- Feel free to rename lenders or debts in a way that reflects your feelings toward them—turn it into a form of financial expression.
- Example: Rename aggressive lenders with humorous or critical names to reflect their impact on your life. It's your list.
- Express your financial situation on your own terms—it's empowering.

Be Specific

- Detail specific debts and shortfalls. For instance, instead of just noting "I have debts," specify exact amounts like "I owe Barclaycard £2,894" or "I owe HSBC credit card £4,000."

- If your expenses exceed your income, clearly state the shortfall, for example, "I need £300 more every month to pay all my bills."

Having this as our first exercise is not just beneficial; it's crucial. It sets the stage for your journey toward financial improvement, giving you a clear understanding of what your financial issues are as you start reading this book.

At this stage, our aim is not to find immediate solutions. It's about acknowledging our financial issues. By taking them out of our minds and writing them out, we can begin to alleviate our worries.

This process not only stops us from dwelling on our problems but also provides a sense of relief. Remember, solutions will come in due time; we have more chapters ahead to guide us.

Congratulations on finishing this exciting first step. Give yourself a pat on the back—you're making progress!

Chapter Two

UNDERSTANDING YOUR FINANCIAL LANDSCAPE

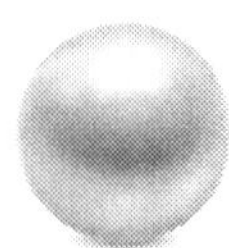

This book began by discussing Black women's unique financial challenges when earning and saving money. Think of every pound that makes it into your bank account as a hard-earned victory over many obstacles. That's why wise money management is crucial to making it last and grow.

Practices like budgeting, saving regularly, investing for the future, and protecting your assets help your money grow and bring you closer to your financial goals. These goals, which are unique to each person, are the building blocks of financial independence. If you haven't set your financial goals yet, don't worry—I'll walk you through how to do this in the coming chapters.

UNDERSTANDING THE CONTROLLABLE AND UNCONTROLLABLE THAT AFFECT YOUR FINANCES

Some money problems are within are control to change. For example, having too much debt, not enough money saved, or spending more than we make, are things we can change. But what about those factors beyond our control? External events can significantly impact your finances, and it's important to be aware of them from the start. Even if financial issues aren't entirely your fault, you are still responsible for addressing them.

Consider the COVID-19 pandemic, a global event that drastically changed how companies operate, affecting jobs across the globe—including mine. During the pandemic, companies faced tough decisions about cost-cutting, which resulted in numerous job losses, disproportionately affecting women of colour (Cox, 2023). This is a real-life example of an external factor beyond individual control that still affects personal finances, illustrating the importance of being prepared for such events.

Inflation: This is when the prices of things go up over time, so your money doesn't buy as much as it used to. The £50 that once covered your weekly groceries barely fills half your shopping basket. In 2023, food prices doubled, making it harder for people to afford basic groceries.

Recession: A recession is a tough time for the economy—almost everyone finds it hard. Here's what usually happens:

- **Businesses worry about making less money.** They aren't sure if they will keep selling their products as usual, so they start making fewer products.
- **Jobs are cut, and hiring stops**. Since businesses make fewer products, they don't need as many people to work for them. This leads to people losing their jobs and companies not hiring new employees.
- **People spend less money**. When people worry about losing their jobs, they cut back on non-essential spending, such as dining out or buying luxury items. For example, if I'm concerned about my finances for the coming month, I might choose to skip my usual visit to the hairdresser. As a result, my hairdresser has fewer clients,

earns less money, and in turn, reduces her own spending because of her reduced income.

- **Governments are under pressure**. With more people out of work, more people need government help, such as unemployment benefits, which puts extra pressure on government resources.

Ronke's story below is an example of how external factors like recession can affect our finances.

Ronke was really good at her job—a total team player who put in long hours. Everyone loved her and wanted her on their team. She made a difficult decision to leave her job due to feeling burned out. The thing is, Ronke made this decision during a recession and didn't realise how hard it would be to find a new job. When she was ready to return to work, finding a suitable role was challenging because companies were not hiring. Ronke spent the following two years job hunting; she used up all her savings and had to move back in with her mum. Even though Ronke was a savvy money manager, not understanding how external economic factors such as a recession could impact her life cost her to use up her entire life savings. If she could go back in time, she would definitely make a different choice. It's a tough lesson to learn.

Global Events: When we hear of major wars and conflicts, we may shrug our shoulders, thinking, well, that war has nothing to do with me, but everyone is affected indirectly. This is especially true if the countries involved in the conflict also happen to be global suppliers. The everyday stuff you buy in your local supermarket becomes more expensive; energy prices may soar, so you must pay more to buy essentials.

Interest Rates: These affect how much you earn on savings and the cost of borrowing money. Higher savings rates mean your money grows faster, while lower borrowing rates make loans cheaper. In reality, banks usually charge higher interest rates for lending money than they pay to individuals for saving money because this is how banks make money.

STAYING ON TOP OF YOUR MONEY GAME

Think about everything you've learned so far. Black women face immense challenges in securing top-paying jobs and advancing their careers. We're underrepresented in boardrooms and often face discrimination and a lack of support in the workplace. When tough times hit, we're the first to feel the impact—whether it's job losses during economic downturns or the overwhelming responsibility of caring for our families.

Because of these challenges, we must be money-mindful. We cannot spend like everyone else. Every penny that finds its way into our accounts has overcome obstacles and hardships. This money is more than just currency; it has survived the fire. It is gold—pure and precious. It's a symbol of our strength and determination as Black women. It deserves to be treated with the utmost care and respect.

As we wrap up our call to financial enlightenment, let us remain dedicated to securing our financial health. When you hear the drums of war in distant lands, don't dismiss them as irrelevant. Ask yourself, 'How will this turmoil impact me?' When whispers of a recession surface, take a moment to consider, "How will this affect my finances? How will rising prices for groceries and utilities stretch my budget?" We must stay alert and ready to respond to the ripples that external events may send across our financial landscapes.

Our journey demands awareness and action. Let's vow never to be caught unprepared. We must educate ourselves, plan with precision, and save with intention. Let's build financial cushions that shield us from unexpected economic storms and invest in our growth to create sustainable wealth. Every decision we make about our money today shapes the future we dream of for ourselves and the generations that follow. This is our power—our control over our financial destiny.

Financial independence isn't just a goal—it's a necessity. Let's move forward confidently, turning every challenge into a stepping stone toward greater financial freedom and security. Together, as a community of strong Black women, let's be unstoppable.

CHAPTER TWO—CORE LESSONS

- Economic forces beyond your control can affect your finances.
- Anticipate and prepare for external economic forces.
- When external chaos arises, ask yourself, "How will this affect me?"
- Build financial cushions to weather unexpected storms.
- Treat every penny you earn with respect—it has fought hard battles to reach you.
- Don't live like everyone else; be mindful of your spending.
- Educate yourself, plan with precision, and save with intention.

Chapter Two—Exercise

Assess Your Income and Expenses

Take a moment to look at your current income and expenses. Are you spending everything you earn as soon as you get it? This exercise is to help you prepare for the unexpected—like sudden increases in costs due to things outside your control. The more money you have left over after paying all your bills, the better prepared you'll be.

If, after doing this exercise, you don't have any money left from your income once all bills are paid, or if your income matches your bills exactly, don't worry too much right now. This is a common issue; we'll work on fixing it together as we progress through this book.

Remember, you've got this!

Chapter Three

FAITH AND MONEY

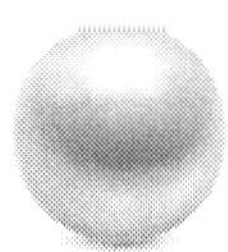

In all my years of exploring personal finance books, I have not seen anything written about faith and money. I get it. It's a touchy subject; many avoid mixing money matters in religious contexts. Yet, we must address it openly, particularly within the UK Black community, where a significant 67% identify as Christian—much higher than the UK's overall 46% (UK Data Service, 2021). Black women make up the majority of churchgoers. This discussion is not just a matter of curiosity but a crucial aspect of your personal finance journey.

This chapter is particularly meaningful for those whose faith includes financial giving as part of worship. While it may resonate most with Christians or those of a religious background, anyone is welcome to explore the insights shared here. If it doesn't align with your beliefs, feel free to move ahead to the next chapter.

Churches often handle substantial sums of money, from regular offerings to members donating a tenth of their income. I have even heard of some churches pressuring members to donate their entire month's earnings as "miracle seeds." Can you imagine how much money that adds up to in a megachurch of thousands?

"Too many churches are mishandling the money that has been entrusted to us" (Vaters, 2018).

Despite the good many churches do; many more behave badly. According to a Christianity Today article, many churches mishandle money entrusted to them. The article goes on to say, "The most widespread sin of the modern-day church is poor stewardship." It's no surprise since the sector remains largely unregulated. It's incredibly easy to start a church. There are no requirements or formal qualifications. Anyone can decide to form a church. I know a few individuals who started churches simply to earn money rather than out of a burning desire to share their faith. The widespread corruption is not surprising. This lack of regulation often leads to financial exploitation within these organisations, and this should not be taken lightly. Ranging from money laundering to the misappropriation of members' donations are major problems in places of worship (Anti-Money Laundering, 2024).

What do you know about how your church handles your donations? Transparency is vital to building trust and ensuring your financial contributions are used as intended.

People from all walks of life attend places of worship. Many come during times of personal crisis, like financial troubles, illness, loss, or major life changes. While places of worship offer comfort and community, there is a risk that individuals who are emotionally or financially vulnerable could be more open to manipulation. This is especially true if they feel that their spiritual well-being is tied to how much they contribute financially.

PROSPERITY GOSPEL 101

Growing up, my life revolved around the church, but money talks were few and far between—with one exception. A recurring message was crystal clear: donate ten per cent of your income, give offerings, and contribute to the church building fund, or live under a curse of poverty.

Scary stuff! I mean, who wants to be cursed?

Squeezing money out of congregants doesn't end with 10% donations. There are numerous other fundraising schemes and numerous ways to collect money from unsuspecting church members, ranging from subtle coercion to outright shaming people to empty their coffers. I've seen people borrowing money just to make a donation.

One memorable encounter occurred when the church I once attended planned to move to a magnificent new church facility. The fundraising spectacle included a video showing the envisioned new building. The congregation was encouraged to dig deep and donate generously.

However, things took a turn when the speaker declared that low or no donations reflected a lack of faith or even defiance of God. And everyone must sow "dangerous seeds." The starting bid was a hefty £10,000. The speaker invited anyone willing to pledge £10,000 to join him at the front. A few hands went up. These courageous individuals were applauded as they walked to the front. They were hailed as "giants of faith." For us, still sitting, the pressure was on.

Gradually, the speaker lowered the pledge amounts, aiming to make the bid accessible to everyone. He was adamant that everyone must pledge, regardless of how much they can afford. All those still seated were jeered and ridiculed until everyone was forced to pledge a minimum of £250.

The experience left me feeling battered and bruised. A place that should have been a safe haven was a breeding ground for exploitation.

The preacher encouraged the congregation to compete with each other in donating to his cause. He promised those who pledged over £1,000 would receive special financial rewards and blessings. He even suggested they would earn extra brownie points and VIP status in God's eyes.

The 'give to get' principle, also known as the 'Prosperity Gospel,' suggests that generous donations will miraculously solve your financial problems and bring you all the wealth you desire. This belief is dangerous because it encourages people to abandon solid financial education, mistaking financial literacy for a lack of faith. Pastors often pressure their congregations to donate on the spot, not giving them time to think it over, likely fearing they'll change their minds if they do. It's concerning that this kind of spiritual manipulation still persists and remains so popular, benefiting those who preach it rather than those who follow it.

TO GIVE OR NOT TO GIVE

- **Understand your scriptures on giving.** Far be it from me to ask you not to give to your religious places of worship. Giving is an act of worship and is highly personal. I would say this: Understand your faith's teachings about money. Sacred texts like the Bible, Torah, and Quran have much to say about money. Do you know what these books teach firsthand? Or is your knowledge based solely on what the preacher tells you? Reading and understanding these texts can empower you to give in a way that aligns with your faith and financial well-being.
- **Seek counsel.** If, after reading, you're still unsure, I encourage you to seek advice from independent and trusted individuals who are knowledgeable about your faith and have nothing to gain from your offerings and donations. Their unbiased advice can help you navigate the complexities of faith and money, ensuring that your contributions align with your beliefs and financial situation.
- **Check with the Charity Commission.** UK churches and other religious groups are often registered charities and must send yearly

financial accounts and reports to the Charity Commission. The reports show how they use member's donations. Asking about these finances helps keep your faith community accountable. If your church isn't registered or you can't find its info online, ask them directly. If they seem uncomfortable or unwilling to answer, be cautious—that's a red flag.

- **God loves a cheerful giver.** Instead of giving because you feel pressured or guilty, give what you've already decided. Be careful of anyone who tries to sweet-talk you into giving more than you can afford. The cold hard fact is this: Dubious pastors have ulterior motives when asking you to donate beyond what you can afford. Your donation pays for their lavish lifestyles. These same pastors don't care if your donations leave you struggling. They will misuse religious texts to convince you, which is why knowing the true meaning and context of scripture quotes can help you spot when you're being manipulated.
- **Beware of fear tactics.** Be wary of leaders who use fear or manipulation to increase donations. True faith should not make you feel threatened or coerced. If promises of instant wealth come with high-pressure donation tactics, that's another red flag.
- **Beware of promises of instant riches.** Again, be cautious. Real financial security comes from careful financial stewardship, consistent saving, and wise investments that grow over time.
- **Lead by example.** Your churches or religious organisations often encourage you to donate generously, but it's crucial that they lead by example in demonstrating true generosity. A church's commitment to generosity should be evident in its local community support. Real generosity means being actively involved in the local area, supporting and uplifting those in need. While foreign missions are commendable, foreign aid should not be the only focus of their charitable efforts. Why? Because charity begins at home. True generosity is visible, consistent, and

integrated into the daily fabric of community life, not just a photo opportunity.

- **Plan ahead**. Use electronic methods like bank transfers if this option is available. This has three benefits:
    - When you plan ahead, you're not just giving on a whim. You've thought about how much you want to give, so you're less likely to be swayed by smooth-talking pastors.
    - Giving electronically leaves a record, which helps keep track of your donations.
    - It's safer for your faith community. Cash donations can be stolen. Also, handling cash takes more time and effort for the religious organisation; you'd be doing them a solid.

In conclusion, faith and money are closely linked, so it's important we don't treat it as a taboo subject. Talk openly and honestly about money. Places of worship should be clear and honest about how they use members' donations. Members should understand what their faith says about money. While donating is a personal act of worship, it shouldn't be forced or manipulated. Give happily, and be proud of the good you do. Remember, only give what you can afford, not what you're pressured to give. Simply handing money to your faith community or sowing "dangerous seeds" won't fix your finances. True financial growth comes from careful financial stewardship, saving wisely, and investing. A woman with a solid money plan will not only grow her wealth well but will also be in a better position to support her religious community and help others.

CHAPTER THREE—CORE LESSONS

- Financial stability involves more than religious giving. Financial peace comes from careful financial stewardship, saving, wise investments, and financial education.

- Be cautious of fear-based tactics used by dodgy leaders when asking for money.
- Exploitative practices exist within religious communities, harm our financial well-being and erode trust in genuine religious institutions.
- Don't let anyone belittle your contributions based on size; every contribution matters.
- Hold your faith communities accountable by ensuring they practice transparency and engage in helpful initiatives within the community.

Chapter Three—Exercise

Understanding the connection between faith and money can be sensitive. You may skip this exercise if you don't practice any specific religion. Alternatively, take a moment to reflect on societal pressures that encourage you to spend money for immediate gain or because you fear negative consequences if you don't comply.

For those who practice a religion and contribute financially, consider reflecting and journaling on the role giving plays in your financial values. How do your religious beliefs impact the way you spend and save money?

Chapter Four

DECODING THE BLACK TAX—A BLESSING OR A BURDEN?

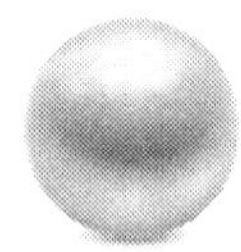

"A rich man with ten poor relatives is a poor man."
—A Yoruba proverb.

This simple yet profound statement encapsulates the essence of the Black Tax—a reality faced by Africans and other Black communities worldwide.

Originally coined in South Africa, it describes the financial obligations individuals abroad and domestically face in supporting their extended families. While helping family is undeniably heartfelt, it often comes with its own set of challenges.

The Black tax goes something like this: A family pools all their resources to send the eldest child overseas for a better education, hoping the child will study hard, complete their education, and then find a well-paying job. Once this child starts working, they are expected to send money back home to support their family. It's like a "return on investment." This financial support might cover everything from household maintenance, educational fees for siblings, and healthcare.

I haven't seen much written about "Black tax," but it is real and profoundly affects people's finances.

Black tax often affects people who are already marginalised, perhaps due to immigration-related concerns and low income. Financially supporting relatives can amount to thousands and may continue for years, even a lifetime. So, navigating this tax without harming our financial future is super-important.

WHAT COULD POSSIBLY GO WRONG?

Wouldn't it be fantastic if young adults could easily send money back to their home countries without any worries? But let's keep it real; living overseas comes with its own set of obstacles.

We've already discussed how challenging it is to find well-paying jobs, especially soon after college. Once your family back home learns that you're working, they begin requesting money. Even if your earnings are modest, it's hard for them to grasp the realities of life abroad.

For example, while £1,000 a month in Lagos, Nigeria, might seem like a lot, it won't cover much in London.

Requests for money come from all directions. In African culture, family isn't limited to immediate relatives; it extends to include grandparents, aunts, uncles, and even distant cousins. With such large families, the need for financial assistance seems never-ending. Everyone wants a share, which can be challenging for individuals already struggling to make ends meet.

A young person works hard and naturally wants to enjoy their earnings—maybe by relaxing with friends or colleagues. They may also want to start building their own life, like saving for emergencies, buying a home, or investing in money-making ventures. However, the heavy demands from back home often prevent them from pursuing any personal financial planning.

Meanwhile, families back home often face genuine and sometimes urgent needs that cannot be ignored. Having lived in Africa, I've experienced the hunger pains firsthand as a child. The challenges are undeniable. So, how does one strike a balance between these two realities without jeopardising their financial stability? This is the crucial question.

My dad was a powerful example of how the 'Black tax' can profoundly impact a life. As the eldest son and a gifted student, he was given the opportunity to study in the United Kingdom in the early 1960s. But life took an unexpected turn when we suddenly had to leave the UK so Dad could return to Nigeria to care for his siblings and relatives. For the next 25 years, supporting them became his life's only mission.

The demands for money were relentless and continued even as Dad grew old and frail. Despite his tireless efforts to help his relatives become self-sufficient, they increasingly leaned on him for their every need, draining every penny he had. Watching him give so much of himself, only to be left with so little, was a heartbreaking reminder of how the weight of family obligations can take a toll on a person's life.

My siblings and I deeply felt the impact of Dad's generosity. While it was admirable how he shared whatever little he had, his generosity put pressure on us. Essentials like school fees often became scarce. Dad would ask us, his children, to go without so his extended family could benefit, always promising to make it up to us later. Although he had the best intentions, this arrangement put a lot of strain on our family dynamic.

Sadly, Dad passed away before my siblings finished school, leaving the burden of the 'Black tax' on my shoulders. As my resources were limited, I was determined not to let history repeat itself, so I took a different approach.

THE DEBATE: IS BLACK TAX A GOOD THING?

I stumbled upon an article titled "Black tax—burden or investment?" and pondered this question. Depending on who you ask, there are compelling arguments for both sides (Dyomfana, 2022).

Arguments for Black Tax

- **Cultural Values**: Many argue that the Black tax is rooted in cultural values of communal support and familial obligation. It's seen as a way for individuals to give back to their families who supported them in their journey to success.
- **Economic Empowerment**: Some proponents of the Black tax believe that financially supporting their families indirectly contributes to the economic empowerment of their communities. This support can help break the cycle of poverty and create opportunities for future generations.
- **Social Cohesion**: Black tax fosters a sense of unity and solidarity within families and communities. It strengthens bonds between relatives and reinforces the importance of mutual support and cooperation.

Arguments Against Black Tax

- **Financial Strain**: Critics believe that the Black tax puts a considerable financial strain on individuals, making it impossible for them to fulfil their financial goals and secure their own futures.

It may limit their ability to save for emergencies, invest, or accumulate wealth.

- **Dependency:** Some argue that the Black tax encourages a culture of reliance, in which family members rely on the financial support of others rather than taking responsibility for their own financial well-being, as was my dad's case. This can keep people trapped in poverty and hold back their personal growth.
- **Freedom to Choose:** Those against Black tax stress the importance of personal freedom and financial independence. They believe everyone should be free to manage their money and focus on their own goals, without feeling pressured to support others.
- **Government Accountability:** When people like us take on the responsibility of supporting our relatives through Black tax, it can reduce the pressure on governments to provide key services like education, healthcare, and social benefits. As a result, public services may become underfunded and inadequate. But what happens to families without children abroad or in big cities? Black tax can make existing inequalities even worse.

Where do I stand on this issue? Well, the Black tax isn't a simple good or bad issue. It's complex. Each situation is different and needs careful consideration.

Take my dad's story, for example. I struggled to find any positives. His unwavering dedication to his extended family left me responsible for supporting my siblings, forcing me to share the little I had. History was repeating itself and played a significant role in my financial struggles. The Black tax clearly has the potential to perpetuate generational poverty. I couldn't turn my back on my siblings—they didn't choose their circumstances. After all, a prosperous Joyce surrounded by struggling siblings isn't truly prosperous. Ignoring their needs would have only led to misery for all of us.

Finding a balance was crucial for me. I approached the Black tax differently, and now my siblings are thriving. This shows that, with the proper management, the Black tax can help break the poverty cycle. Our younger generation won't have to carry this burden—poverty cycle is broken.

But my heart aches for those still trapped as many endure the Black tax for a lifetime, unable to lift their families out of poverty. The struggle is real. Consider these harsh realities:

- One in three people in Africa lives below the global poverty line (Hamel et al., 2019). Well-managed assistance via Black tax to our carefully selected relatives can break the chain of poverty.
- Eighty per cent of Africa's elderly population faces the harsh reality of no pension, condemning them to a life of poverty in an unforgiving climate (ILO, 2014). This is why we cannot abandon our elders.
- Over 615 million Africans lack access to free essential healthcare services (AHAIC, 2025). There is no NHS out there. The help received as Black tax can be the difference between life and death.
- Sub-Saharan Africa has the highest rate of education exclusion in the world (UNESCO, 2018). As in, children in Africa lack access to quality education. Education is the key to breaking the cycle of poverty. The more education they receive, the better their chances of escaping poverty.

NAVIGATING THE BLACK TAX WITHOUT HARMING YOUR FINANCIAL FUTURE

So, given the complexity of this topic, how can we continue to empower our relatives without jeopardising our financial security and growth opportunities?

Get Your Finances in Order: Start by taking control of your current financial situation. Understand your income and expenses—do you have money left after covering your essentials? Are your emergency savings in place? Debt—are you struggling with it or debt-free? Remember, you should only give from your surplus. Make sure you're financially stable before helping others. Think of it like a flight's safety instructions—secure your mask before assisting others. By prioritising your financial well-being, you'll be better equipped to offer meaningful and sustainable support to your loved ones.

Empower Through Education: Imagine working hard to manage your money wisely, only to watch it disappear in the hands of relatives who can't stop splurging. Instead of just handing out cash, why not teach your relatives how to manage their money? Help them see the importance of living within their means and saving for the future. If they still ignore these lessons, take action—don't fuel wasteful habits. Tighten the purse strings. Giving money might solve the problem for a moment, but teaching financial skills creates lasting stability and success.

Be Open and Honest: Honesty is key when helping family members. Don't overstate your financial situation just to impress. Be upfront about what you can truly afford. It's easy to fall into the trap of giving just to show off or outdo others. I've seen people give, not out of abundance, but to prove they have what others don't. Check your motives. Instead, focus on giving within your means. Being clear about your finances sets healthy boundaries and helps your family seek support elsewhere if needed.

Create Income-Generating Assets: The best way to help family members is by setting them up with something that makes money on its own. It's a way to help them stand on their own two feet. Covering things like food and rent is a slippery slope—once you start, it never ends. You're basically encouraging them to rely on you for everything. Unless it's for elderly or disabled relatives, avoid paying for everyday needs. Even with elderly relatives, putting your money into something that can generate income to support them long-term is a better way to go.

Crocs and Lizards: "A lizard in Nigeria will not become a crocodile in London." You can't help everyone. No matter how much money you have, the demands will always exceed your resources. So, how do you navigate this? Think of it like this: crocodiles and lizards may look similar when they hatch, but one grows large while the other stays small. Not everyone you help will give you the same return on your investment. Be selective in your choices. Support those who are driven and likely to make your help count —the Crocs.

Remember that sibling story from the first chapter? It's crystal clear—Zuri is the croc, and Akello, the lizard. Investing in Zuri is the smart play. Think of it like the selection process on TV shows like The Apprentice or Dragon's Den—they pick the best candidate. Look for the brightest, the most ambitious, and the ones who hustle. Age and gender shouldn't dictate your choice; hunger and drive should.

Don't throw your money around blindly—focus on those with real potential for success. Assess the likelihood of a positive outcome before you invest in a business venture. Your relatives might not always agree with your decisions, but remember, you've earned that money through hard work. Anyone wanting your money must prove they can turn it into more. Your money is valuable—make sure it's in the right hands.

Encourage Family Collaboration: Encourage your family to rally together toward common objectives. Avoid the "every man for himself" mindset. Highlight the strength and solidarity that come from collective effort. This strategic approach yields numerous benefits:

- Make the best use of the money available. If you are the only provider, the funds will be limited, so the little available money mustn't be squandered on pipe dreams.
- Don't bite off more than you can chew. Stretching yourself thin only leads to burnout and financial strain.

- Your family can focus on and pursue larger financial goals, such as buying property or starting a family business that will benefit the whole family.
- Beyond the money aspect, your family can strengthen bonds and create a more supportive network.

As we wrap up, here's what I want to leave you with: **The Black tax is a temporary way to help lift your family out of poverty.** Set clear boundaries with a start and end date for your financial help, and communicate this openly with your family. Focus on helping them become self-sufficient rather than creating long-term dependence. Most importantly, while supporting others, don't forget about your own financial health—**you matter too**.

CHAPTER FOUR—CORE LESSONS

- **Temporary Solution:** Black tax involves financial support for relatives, but it should be seen as a temporary solution to empower them and escape poverty.
- **Financial Clarity:** Gain a clear understanding of your financial situation, including income, expenses, and savings.
- **Empowerment Through Education:** Educate relatives on financial management to instil lifelong skills rather than temporary solutions.
- **Honesty and Boundaries:** Maintain honesty about your financial capacity and set clear boundaries to manage expectations.
- **Family Unity:** Foster a collaborative approach within the family to maximise resources and achieve collective goals.
- **Long-Term Empowerment:** Provide structured assistance with defined timelines to empower loved ones to stand independently
- **Advocacy for Change:** Advocate for systemic changes to address the underlying issues contributing to the Black tax burden.

Chapter Four—Exercise

Reflective Journaling: Think back on your experiences with supporting family members financially. Consider moments where you may have faced challenges or felt overwhelmed by the responsibility. Did you encounter situations where providing tough love could have led to positive changes or improvements in your family dynamic?

Use this opportunity to explore your feelings and thoughts about family financial support. Write down your reflections, insights, and any actions you may want to take to ensure a healthy balance between supporting your loved ones and safeguarding your financial well-being.

Chapter Five

THE WEALTH GPS—MAPPING YOUR FINANCIAL FUTURE

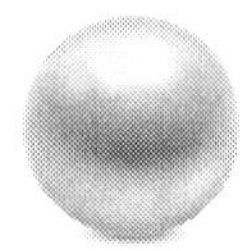

"Ah, setting financial goals–a topic often met with eye rolls and dismissed as a cliché. But hold on; overlooking this step is like going on a journey without a destination. Picture wandering endlessly in the wilderness of desperation, squandering valuable time and scarce resources.

Let me not get ahead of myself here. Think of SMART financial goals like the GPS of the satnav in your car that will take you from where you are currently with your money to where you want to be. SMART is an acronym made up of:

- Specific
- Measurable
- Achievable
- Relevant
- Time-Bound

My friend, setting SMART financial goals is a crucial and straightforward process that steers us toward a brighter financial future. Dee, a client, walked into my office, burdened with debt but determined to become debt-free. "Joyce, I want to clear this debt by August 2018 and start saving for my home by September 2018." Voilà! Dee set her SMART financial goals; unaware she was doing so because it is so easy. Dee's goal was SMART because it was specific and time-bound—concepts we'll discuss in more detail in a moment.

But first, let me share four simple reasons why embracing financial goals is pivotal for your success:

- **Focus:** Financial goals act like a target, keeping you on track and preventing unnecessary spending. For instance, aiming to save for your first home makes you less likely to splurge on less vital expenses.
- **Reduce Stress:** Having a goal removes financial stress, providing a sense of direction and control over your finances.
- **Achievement:** Achieving financial goals is immensely rewarding—a testament to your hard work and discipline.
- **Plan for the Future:** Goals prompt long-term thinking, whether buying a house, retiring comfortably, or funding major life events.

WHY YOUR MONEY DESERVES SMART TREATMENT

Let's rewind to the opening chapter of this book. Remember the exercise where we jotted down all those financial woes? Now's the moment to re-visit them. If you haven't done it yet, no worries —just flip back to Chapter One's exercise and catch up. It's the perfect time to peek into that list and shape those woes into SMART goals.

If one of your items screams "debt," consider transforming that into a SMART goal. For someone facing a credit card debt of £20,000, let's break it down using the SMART acronym:

S = Specific: Get crystal clear about what you want to achieve. Instead of a vague "I want to be debt-free," aim for something specific like "I want to pay off £20,000 in two years."

M = Measurable: Numbers matter here. Make it quantifiable and trackable. For instance, a measurable goal might be "I will pay £833 toward clearing my credit card debt each month." Numbers don't lie; checking progress against this goal is easy. In other words, £833 X 24 months equates to £20,000.

A = Achievable: Reality check time! Make sure your goal is realistic and within reach. For example, paying off £20,000 in two years is more manageable for some than others. The more disposable income you have, the easier it is to achieve. However, most people who are starting to fix their finances typically don't have much extra money. In that case, instead of aiming to pay off £833 a month on a £2,000 salary, set a more realistic goal like £500 or less per month. Don't overwhelm yourself–keep it achievable.

There's often a strong urge to rush when taking control of our finances. After neglecting them for years, it's natural to feel behind and rush to tackle debts, savings, and investments simultaneously. But remember, slow and steady wins the race. Trust the process; steady progress will get you there without the frustration and overwhelm of moving too quickly.

R = Relevant: Build with purpose. In this example, clearing the debt should connect to the bigger financial picture. Dee's goal of becoming debt-free ties directly to her plans to save up and buy a home. Achieving the first goal is key to making the next two possible. You see what I mean?

T = Time-Bound: The clock is ticking! Setting deadlines injects urgency and prevents procrastination. For instance, someone aiming to clear a £20,000 debt in two years should check their progress every six months. By the six-month mark, they should have paid off £5,000, allowing them to adjust their strategy if needed.

THE SMART TURNAROUND

I believe this chapter wouldn't be complete without a real-life example illustrating what setting SMART goals really means:

At 29, my financial situation was chaotic. I had a ton of debt and was spending more than I earned, which frustrated me. So, as someone passionate about personal finance, I set a goal:

It was simple.

I must be a millionaire by age 40. I remember feeling very pleased as I envisioned my massive mansion on a tropical island, somewhere hot and sunny with lots and lots of palm trees. And, me sitting on the beach sipping a cocktail.

By age 40, I was nowhere close to being a millionaire. In fact, my finances were worse. So, what went wrong?

Well, my goal wasn't SMART.

Let's deconstruct this for a moment:

- **Specific:** Yes, aiming for a million was a specific number, but it wasn't specific enough. What did "being a millionaire" really mean? Having a million dollars in my bank account? Having a net worth of a million dollars? I'm not sure that I even really knew specifically what I wanted when I declared this goal.
- **Measurable:** Nope, my goal was not measurable. While one million is a number to measure, I didn't track progress or set achievable steps. For instance, I could've aimed for £100,000 in the first year. I never broke down how I would measure my progress along the way, so the goal was ambiguous.

- **Achievable:** My goal was definitely not achievable. My earnings were far below what was needed, even with an ideal career progression.
- **Relevant:** Nope, again—not relevant. My resources didn't match my dream. I was just relying on the single income from my job, which had no way of getting me to the goal I'd set. The goal was more of a pipe dream, which was irrelevant to the situation I was in.
- **Time-Bound:** Eleven years was a time constraint, sure, but just like being measurable, I didn't track time-bound progress or set achievable landmarks along the way, such as six-month or one-year increments for saving. The timeline was too ambiguous to be actionable.

Looking back, the goal of a million was wishful thinking. But I learned and revamped my approach. These were my new goals:

Goal 1: To align my expenses with my income and ensure I stop spending more than I earn. To achieve this, I meticulously combed through every expense, striving to bring them down until they matched or were less than my monthly income.

Goal 2: To save up an emergency fund of at least £500, and I successfully achieved this milestone within just three months.

Goal 3: To be debt-free within three years, and I nailed it. I have to admit that the first goal of cutting costs played a crucial role in making Goals 2 and 3 a reality.

As I achieve my goals, new ones crop up. My ultimate goal is to generate sufficient passive income, freeing me from the constraints of a 9-to-5 job that's here today but gone tomorrow. To spend quality time with loved ones. To support causes close to my heart and embark on adventures, exploring new and exciting places.

Your goals will evolve over time, and it's essential to have short-, medium-, and long-term objectives. The shorter- and medium-term goals should align with and contribute to the long-term goals.

Having multiple goals is perfectly fine as long as they are manageable. Avoid overwhelming yourself, and as you accomplish one goal, set new ones using the SMART framework.

In conclusion, setting SMART financial goals is like navigating with a GPS for your money, guiding you from where you are to where you want to be. It's not just about dreams; it's actionable steps toward financial freedom. By focusing on Specific, Measurable, Achievable, Relevant, and Time-Bound goals, you gain clarity, reduce stress, celebrate achievements, and plan for the future. Remember, slow and steady wins the race, and as your goals evolve, trust the SMART framework to keep you on track.

CHAPTER FIVE—CORE LESSONS

- Setting financial goals becomes simple with the SMART framework: Specific, Measurable, Achievable, Relevant, and Time-Bound.
- Focus on the aspect of your finances causing distress and set clear objectives.
- Dream big, but ensure your goals align with your current resources and capabilities.
- Avoid overwhelming yourself; focus on achievable targets.
- Goals will change over time; adapt to new circumstances.
- As you achieve goals, add new ones using the SMART framework.
- Ensure shorter-term goals contribute to and align with longer-term objectives.

- Reflect on past goals that weren't SMART to improve future goal setting.
- Adapt and revamp past financial goals according to the SMART framework.

Chapter Five—Exercise

Take a look at the most urgent money issues on your list. Plan how to solve them by setting SMART goals—Specific, Measurable, Achievable, Relevant, and Time-Bound. Keep it simple, and enjoy the process.

All the best; I am rooting for you.

Chapter Six

YOUR UNIQUE MONEY PERSONALITY

Think of your money personality as how you naturally handle money—your personal money blueprint. Understanding it can unlock the key to your financial success.

In this chapter, we'll explore different money personalities, how our background shapes them, and how they impact our financial health. By understanding our money habits, we'll see our strengths and, of course, areas for improvement.

SPENDERS

A spender is an individual who derives pleasure from immediate gratification and tends to enjoy indulging in purchases and experiences. They have a mindset of "living in the moment" and may prioritise enjoying life's pleasures over long-term financial security. Spenders often find it challenging to resist impulse buying and may struggle with managing their finances effectively. They may be prone to accumulating debt and have difficulty saving for the future.

INVESTORS

Investors take a long-term view of their finances and focus on growth opportunities. They are willing to take calculated risks when investing their money. They understand the importance of having different types of investments in their portfolios. They may allocate a portion of their income toward investments such as stocks, real estate, or mutual funds.

AVOIDERS

An avoider is an individual who tends to shy away from dealing with financial matters. They may avoid tasks such as budgeting, financial discussions, or even opening bills. Avoiders often feel overwhelmed or anxious about money and may engage in avoidance behaviours as a coping mechanism. This can lead to financial disorganisation, missed opportunities, and a lack of financial progress. Avoiders may benefit from support and education to overcome their avoidance tendencies and build healthy financial habits.

SAVERS

Savers have a strong tendency to save money and are cautious when it comes to spending money. They are financially disciplined. They budget, set financial goals, and stick to them. They have money saved for emergencies and avoid debt. Wow, that sounds perfect, right? Well, being a saver is good, but they could do better. Savers are overly risk-averse. They don't take even the smallest risk, which means they don't grow their wealth through investments. They are satisfied with low returns on their savings.

HOARDERS

Hoarders take saving to the extreme. They accumulate money without a purpose and store it away, rarely spending or investing. They fear parting with money and would rather suffer than use the money to improve their quality of life or benefit others. Hoarders are overly frugal and miss out on enjoyable life experiences because they're reluctant to spend. I grew up with real-life hoarders. They are not fun to be around!

MONEY PERSONALITIES IN REAL LIFE

I invite you to embark on a journey that uncovers the profound influence of our financial behaviours and attitudes. Through the stories of four friends—Fatima, Ada, Kayin, and Mariam—we will gain a deeper understanding of the varied money personalities and how they can shape our lives.

These individuals represent different aspects of our experiences, shedding light on the complex relationship between our upbringing, mindset, and financial habits.

Fatima The Spender: Meet Fatima, the life of the party, whose infectious energy and generosity light up any room she enters. She's the friend who goes above and beyond to make everyone feel special. But behind her cheerful façade lies a hidden struggle.

Fatima's journey began with humble beginnings. Raised as the youngest of five children of an immigrant family, she grew up poor. Despite the hardships of her upbringing, she's carved out a successful career as a PA at a posh London bank, enjoying a comfortable salary. Yet, despite her generous salary, she's haunted by a feeling that there's just never enough money for everything she wants.

Whenever Fatima gets money, she spends it as soon as it lands in her account for fear that the money will vanish because of the constant needs of her demanding family members. Buying things makes her feel happy. She is now living the life she fantasised about as a child. Saving money or planning for the future is not a high priority. She thinks she can't afford to save yet because there are so many things she needs.

Fatima distances herself from her impoverished past. She moved as far away as possible from home to the most opulent part of town. But this pursuit of luxury comes with a hefty price tag, as her exorbitant rent takes up a significant portion of her monthly earnings. Her lavish apartment, adorned with expensive trinkets, was all purchased on credit. She's now having trouble keeping up with the payments.

Fatima loves treating herself, but her financial stability is in danger because she owes a lot of money and might not be able to keep up her appearance when the debt collectors come knocking.

Fatima's story shows how spending too much can cause problems, and it's essential to find a balance between enjoying life and being smart with money.

SOLUTIONS FOR FATIMA AND OTHERS LIKE HER

- **Embrace Change:** For Fatima, there has to be a genuine desire to change and be free of financial stress. Change is challenging and sometimes downright painful. But remaining stagnant is equally, if not more, challenging. It's a catch-22 situation—damned if you do, damned if you don't. Life presents challenges regardless of whether we choose to stay stagnant or face our battles.

  However, there's a distinction between good and bad pain. The pain of remaining the same, stuck in a cycle of overspending and financial stress, versus the pain of facing one's battles and overcoming them. While the pain of change may seem daunting, it ultimately leads to growth and financial freedom. Embracing the discomfort of change and the challenge of reshaping spending habits into saving habits leads to a brighter financial future. In the end, the pain of change is always better than the pain of remaining stagnant.

- **Set New Goals:** Fatima can set goals for her financial future. As someone who tends to spend freely, her goals may involve breaking the habit of overspending and instead focusing on saving. Envisioning a stress-free life devoid of money worries is a powerful exercise for her.

- **Use Financial Control Tools:** Here's a summary of the action plan for Fatima:
    - **Budgeting**: Create a detailed budget to track income and expenses. This will help her clearly understand her financial situation and whether she's spending more than she earns.
    - **Expense Tracking**: Track spending in various categories to identify where most of her money goes and pinpoint areas where she can cut costs.
    - **Control Spending**: Ensure spending does not exceed income. This may involve Fatima adjusting her spending habits and reducing unnecessary expenses.
    - **Start Saving**: This would involve setting aside a portion of Fatima's monthly income toward savings goals, such as building an emergency fund or saving for future expenses.

- **Recognise Emotional Triggers:** Fatima must understand the emotions driving her spending habits. A challenging childhood often triggers undesirable financial habits, and incidents buried in our subconscious mind can sometimes lead to irrational spending patterns.

Real-Life Example: I never thought of myself as a spender, but I had a thing for shoes that I couldn't shake—I loved buying shoes. I'd buy the same pair in different colours. It took some deep thinking to figure out why. As a child, I only ever had one pair of shoes at a time for everything—school, church, and parties. One day, I lost my only pair. They were new, and I dreaded asking my parents for a replacement. So, I went barefoot for a while. The shame and embarrassment of going barefoot stuck with me and drove my endless desire for shoes in adulthood. Realising this was a breakthrough that helped me curb my shoe-buying habit. The point of this story is that it's crucial to understand why we overspend and uncover the past or present issues driving our behaviour.

For instance, many people spend money because society promotes a Eurocentric beauty ideal, pressuring us to buy products that promise to 'fix' our perceived flaws. In the report 'Black Women's Body Image,' Kelch-Oliver & Ancis (2011) discuss how outdated stereotypes, like the 'tragic mulatto' and the preference for lighter-skinned Black women, keep these beauty standards alive. As a result, Black women often feel pressured to alter their natural appearance to fit in, leading to significant spending on products to achieve this goal. Let me ask you this: Have you ever watched a YouTube video promoting an ideal hair type and ended up buying everything the influencer claimed to use? I know I have. I have a shelf full of unused hair products to prove it.

High-end brands market their products as symbols of success and status, playing on our insecurities about social standing and self-worth. For Black women, who often have to fight harder for recognition and respect, buying these brands can feel like a way to show our achievements, even if it costs us financially. I've seen Black women borrow money to buy designer items, thinking they'll be more respected when decked out in designer gear. For us, it's often more than just feeling or looking good; we often buy these expensive items to prove a point—that we are as successful as others.

Even something as simple as education can be a trigger. I know many Black women who are forever students, paying high fees just to feel "good enough." They think, "If I could just get that extra qualification, then I would be promoted," or "If I could just complete that certification, then I would be seen as competent."

Understanding these triggers and how they affect us is the first step towards breaking free from these spending habits. By looking at the root causes of our financial behaviours, we can make better decisions and empower ourselves to spend in ways that genuinely reflect our values and goals.

Ada The Investor: Ada grew up in a low- to moderate-income family with her mum, Ajoke, a hardworking single parent. Ajoke instilled financial discipline in Ada, teaching her valuable lessons about money. From a young age, Ada learned the importance of living within one's means, saving for rainy days, and even investing, no matter how small the amounts. These lessons became the foundation of Ada's financial wisdom.

During her secondary school years, Ada made a smart move. Instead of spending her dinner money on ready meals at school, she brought food from home and saved the cash in the savings account her mum had opened for her since birth. This early habit of saving laid the groundwork for her financial success.

As she pursued her education at university, Ada continued to make wise choices. She worked while studying, determined to avoid accumulating a massive student loan debt. Her commitment to financial responsibility was evident even in her early twenties.

Once she started her career, Ada wasted no time. At just 23 years old, she began saving in her employer's pension scheme. She understood the importance of planning for her future.

Ada's financial prowess didn't stop there. She seized the opportunity to contribute to the government's tax-free savings, ensuring she took full advantage of the yearly allowance. And recently, she achieved another significant milestone—buying a buy-to-let property in her old university town. She's eager to boost her income through rental earnings from this property.

Now, you might wonder, "What can I do if I didn't grow up with good money role models or if I didn't have much money during my childhood?" Well, it's never too late to develop good financial habits.

PRACTICAL STEPS TO DEVELOP GOOD FINANCIAL HABITS

1. **Live below your means**. Make a budget that allows you to spend less than you earn. Avoid getting swept away by consumer culture that often fills our homes with stuff but empties our hearts and pockets. Seek emotional value in experiences and relationships, not just in material possessions. Breaking free from consumer culture starts with understanding that your worth isn't defined by what you own but by who you are.
2. **Cultivate saving habits**. Regardless of your past, start saving now. Even small amounts can add up over time. Open a savings account and commit to regular deposits. The amounts you save do not matter as much as consistently putting money in your savings. Resist and do not withdraw money from your savings.
3. **Build an emergency fund**. Aim for at least three months' worth of living expenses. This safety net can protect you during unexpected financial setbacks like a loss of income.
4. **Educate yourself about investing.** Even if you're starting with small sums, consider options like low-cost index funds. An index fund is like a basket of all the top companies in the stock market. Instead of picking individual stocks, you invest in the whole

market, spreading the risk. Low-cost index funds are great because they're cheap and often perform well over time. Once you've saved for your short-term needs, consider index funds to grow your money steadily with less effort.

Ada's story shows that good financial habits can be learned and practised at any stage in life. Start today, and you'll be on your way to a more secure financial future.

Kayin The Avoider: Kayin embodies many traits of the avoider money personality, shaped by a chaotic upbringing where financial irresponsibility was the norm. Her parents' careless approach to money led to eviction and homelessness when she was just a little girl, casting a shadow of financial uncertainty over her life.

Kayin's avoider tendencies manifest in several ways: she often ignores bills, avoids checking bank statements, and postpones critical financial decisions. Lacking basic financial knowledge, she struggles with concepts like budgeting, saving, and investing.

The fear of financial responsibilities, inherited from her parents, makes managing money overwhelming and stressful. She avoids discussing finances, even with close friends like Ada, the financial Wizkid, or her financially responsible uncle John. Money conversations make her anxious and uncomfortable.

Kayin doesn't engage in long-term financial planning and lacks clear goals or a retirement plan. When she does handle money, it's often impulsive, leading to unchecked spending and ignored credit card bills. Despite her past, Kayin's story doesn't have to end in despair. She has the potential to confront her financial fears and take control of her situation. Here's how she can turn things around.:

SOLUTIONS FOR KAYIN AND OTHER AVOIDERS

1. **Own your fear about money.** The fear and anxiety that avoiders like Kayin feel is real. Some people just hate the sight of a spreadsheet or lots of numbers on a page. Be kind and true to yourself by acknowledging this fear. Since money is a big part of adult life, we cannot ignore money. Seek help from people you love and trust who happen to be good with money. It is essential to choose people who will not judge you or make you feel worse. In Kayin's case, her friend Ada or her uncle John will be ideal candidates.
2. **Get basic financial education.** Kayin can start by educating herself about personal finance. There are many beginner-friendly resources available online, like articles, videos, and courses, to help her build a solid financial foundation.
3. **Seek professional help.** If her financial situation is complex, Kayin can consider seeking advice from her bank. Personal bankers see so many money situations on a daily basis; they are skilled to help, and they are less likely to judge. They can teach you how to budget and encourage saving habits. The service is free. Being good with money is in your bank's best interest. Seek their help.

Mariam The Saver/Hoarder: Mariam is a saver bordering on a hoarder personality, shaped by her upbringing in a family that valued impressing others and keeping up appearances. Her mum had a thing for expensive designer clothes, while her dad was all about cars and gadgets. Dad fancied himself as a savvy investor, but in reality, he often took risks with their money, leading to significant losses over the years.

Mariam observed her parents' money mistakes. And, heaven forbid, she follows in her parent's footsteps by spending lavishly on clothes and gadgets just to show off. Instead, she's happy to shop very occasionally at her local thrift shop.

Her budgeting skills are top-notch, diligently tracking her income and expenses. Building an emergency fund is a priority for her, ensuring she's ready for unexpected expenses.

Mariam avoids credit cards like the plague. She doesn't take any risks with her money, keeping all her savings in an account that pays no interest. She has no goal for her money and is not concerned about making big profits; her main goal is to keep her money safe, remembering how her father's risky investments caused the family to lose money.

Mariam has never been abroad and frequently declines to go on holiday with her friends because she'd rather save her money. It does not end there; she seldom joins her friends for a girls' night out unless the event is held at home with very little expense, much to the frustration of her friends.

Being a saver is a good money trait, but it can be even better. Savers like Mariam can explore opportunities to make more from their money by investing in low-risk options. Here's how she can do it:

SOLUTIONS FOR MARIAM AND OTHER SAVERS

1. **High-Yield Savings Accounts**: Mariam can consider moving her savings to high-yield savings accounts, which offer better interest rates. This way, she can earn more without taking big risks.
2. **Government Bonds**: Government bonds are secure investment options. Mariam can look into options like Treasury bonds, which provide reliable super low-risk returns over time.
3. **Diversified Low-Risk Investments:** Mariam can explore diversified, low-risk investments like index funds or bond funds. These let her grow her money while keeping it safe.
4. **Selective Spending**: Mariam should work to understand that while saving is instrumental to future success, she also deserves

to spend a small amount of her hard-earned money. Mariam can choose one or two treats per year to reward herself for her diligent work and saving.

By finding a balance between saving and low-risk investing, Mariam can secure her financial future without repeating her parents' financial mistakes.

MASTERING THE MIX: COMBINING TRAITS FOR FINANCIAL FREEDOM

Each of us has small amounts of spender, investor, avoider, saver, and hoarder traits, but typically, one trait dominates. What do you believe to be your defining trait?

Now, if you're hoping to achieve financial independence—and who isn't? —the secret is to combine elements of savers and investors with a pinch of spender for enjoyment. This combo sets you up for growth while also ensuring you're prepared for whatever life throws your way. Treating yourself every now and then is essential for happiness, but splurging too much can derail your financial goals. Find the balance between enjoying life while still saving and investing for the future.

Recognising your money personality type helps you pinpoint your areas of strength and growth. With some financial know-how and determination, you can change your money personality to match your goals.

To wrap up, understanding your money personality is key to financial success. These traits can change with life events, learning, and personal growth. Stay open to change, and you'll set yourself up for financial improvement.

So, what's your money personality? And what steps will you take to shape your financial destiny?

CHAPTER SIX—CORE LESSONS

- Money personalities are unique traits that influence attitudes, actions, and decision-making regarding money.
- Understanding your money personality is essential for unlocking the secret to financial success.
- The prominent money personalities are Spenders, Investors, Avoiders, and Savers/Hoarders.
- Spenders enjoy immediate gratification, struggle with impulse buying, and find it hard to manage finances effectively.
- Investors take a strategic approach, seek long-term growth, and prioritise investing for the future.
- Avoiders shy away from financial matters, leading to disorganisation and missed opportunities.
- Savers/Hoarders prioritise saving but may struggle to balance saving and enjoying resources.
- Understanding money personalities helps identify strengths, weaknesses, and areas for growth.
- Money personalities can change over time due to life events and personal growth.
- Cultural and societal factors can shape attitudes and beliefs about money.

Chapter Six—Exercise

Reflection Journaling: Keep a reflection journal where you can explore your attitudes, beliefs, and experiences related to money.

Answer these thought-provoking questions and gain insights into your financial mindset:

1. What is your earliest money memory? How did that memory shape your current money personality and habits?
2. Identify your biggest financial triumph and challenge. How does your money personality play a role?
3. Picture your ideal relationship with money. How does it match up with your current money personality? Create a plan to close the gap and bring your finances into alignment.
4. Recall a recent financial regret. How did your money personality influence the decision? Reflect on what you've learned from this regret and how you will act differently for future choices.
5. Observe others' different money approaches. What lessons can you learn from their approaches, and how might you apply them for personal financial growth?

Chapter Seven

BUILDING FINANCIALLY HEALTHY RELATIONSHIPS

The most important financial decision you will ever make is who you choose as your life partner. Your path to wealth will either be helped or hindered by the partner you choose. So, choose wisely.

In his book *Why Didn't They Teach Me This in School?* Cary Siegal bluntly states, "Marry the financially right person." I couldn't agree more.

According to a study by Ramsey Solutions, money is the number one issue married couples fight about, and it's consistently a leading cause of divorce (Ramsey, 2021). That's why being on the same page financially from the onset is essential for a strong, lasting partnership. We must proactively consider financial compatibility.

Each of us has our own money mindset, which is shaped by our upbringing and experiences. We also bring financial baggage into relationships. Understanding these differences is vital to avoiding money conflicts. Our financial journey becomes smoother when our money values match our partners'. But when there's a mismatch, it can lead to tension and instability.

In many African and Black communities, there's often a strong emphasis on spiritual compatibility. While this is important, it's equally crucial to consider financial compatibility, especially considering that many couples cite money as a leading cause of divorce.

Patriarchy often reinforces old-school gender roles, where men usually hold the reins over the money. For Black women, picking a partner on the same financial page can take the sting out of these outdated norms. Seeing eye-to-eye on money matters cuts down on arguments and fights, making for a smoother relationship.

Imagine this scenario: in a heterosexual relationship, the wife loves to save, while the husband prefers to spend. Since men are often seen as the head of the household, they usually have the final say. The wife's attempts to save might be viewed as a lack of submission. If she's the higher earner, God help her! Her sensible approach to saving could be wrongly seen as trying to control him or flaunt her earnings. I've seen this kind of drama unfold more than a few times in close quarters. Save yourself the trouble by making sure you and your partner are financially aligned from the start.

UNDERSTANDING YOUR PARTNER'S FINANCIAL VIEWS

The previous chapter explored how different money mindsets influence financial behaviours and attitudes. These mindsets, shaped by our upbringing, culture, and past experiences, form our 'money personality.' By now, you should have a solid understanding of your money personality type.

Now that you're familiar with your own money personality, it's important to consider that your partner also has their unique money personality. Sometimes, these personalities can clash. Understanding your money personality is one thing, but navigating your partner's money personality adds another layer of complexity to your relationship. The good news is that your money personality isn't set in stone, nor is your partner's. The key is for your partner to recognise their money personality and be open to change if needed.

Your partner might not be familiar with money personalities—they haven't read this book, after all. Rather than grilling them about finances on the first few dates—which might understandably freak them out—observe their money habits. Their behaviour will reveal more than a list of questions ever could. Notice how they handle money during a night out; it can offer valuable clues about their money personality. Direct questions early on can make people defensive, causing them to hide their true financial habits. Focus on their actions rather than their words to understand their approach to money management and how well your financial attitudes align.

But there comes a point in a committed relationship where asking questions becomes necessary.

Financial success typically hinges on a few fundamental principles. Your questions should centre around these principles:

- Spending less than you earn.
- Regularly saving to create a financial cushion.
- Growing wealth through investments.
- Minimising reliance on debt.
- Maintaining a good credit score
- Periodically reviewing your finances to stay on track with your goals.

Here's a list of questions to kickstart discussions about finances and assess compatibility in this vital aspect of your relationship:

1. What are your short-term and long-term financial goals?
2. How do you approach budgeting and managing expenses?

3. What is your attitude toward debt, and do you have any outstanding debts?
4. How do you handle unexpected expenses or emergencies?
5. What are your views on saving money, and do you have a savings strategy?
6. Are you comfortable discussing financial matters openly and transparently?
7. How do you feel about joint finances versus maintaining separate accounts?
8. What are your thoughts on investing, and do you have any investment portfolios?
9. How do you prioritise spending, and what are your most significant financial priorities?
10. How do you plan to handle major financial decisions or purchases as a couple?
11. What role do you believe generosity toward extended family should play in your financial plans?
12. Have you experienced any significant financial setbacks or challenges in the past, and if so, how did you overcome them?
13. How do you envision your financial future individually and as a couple?
14. Are you open to seeking financial advice or counselling if needed?
15. How do you balance your financial responsibilities with your personal and leisure spending habits?

There are many more questions you can ask; this list is not exhaustive.

OBSERVING YOUR PARTNER'S FAMILY FINANCIAL HABITS

It's not just your partner's money-handling skills that matter. Their family's financial habits can also give you valuable insights.

We often learn from what we see our parents do. If your partner's parents are savvy savers, it's likely your partner picked up some good habits. On the other hand, if financial chaos is the norm in their household, it's worth paying attention to how that might affect your partner's approach to money.

Observing your partner's relatives can reveal a lot. Do they openly discuss financial goals and challenges? Is there a sense of financial stability or constant stress about money? These observations can help you understand your partner better and anticipate potential financial habits that might impact your relationship.

Of course, you are not there to judge or make assumptions but rather to gain a fuller picture of what financial habits may have been passed down. By being observant and open about these insights, you can work together to build healthy financial habits as a couple.

HAVING THE MONEY TALK

Talking about money in a relationship can be very difficult. There's a natural fear of potentially disrupting the harmony of the relationship or even risking it altogether. However, it's important to recognise that having open and honest conversations about finances is not just vital; it's a bond-strengthening exercise because it builds a solid foundation for your partnership, A foundation rooted in trust and understanding. Here are some ways to bring up these issues without causing unnecessary tension:

- **Choose the Right Time:** Timing is critical when starting discussions about finances. It's best to choose a moment when you are both relaxed and free from distractions. Avoid bringing up these topics during heated arguments or stressful situations.
- **Start Early:** Ideally, money discussions should begin early in the relationship, during the dating phase. This allows you to gauge

your compatibility and assess whether your financial goals align. However, it's never too late to start if you're already in a committed relationship and haven't had these discussions yet.

- **Frame It Positively:** Approach the conversation with a positive and non-confrontational attitude. Express your desire to better understand your partner's financial values and goals, emphasising that it is essential to building a solid relationship.
- **Be Vulnerable:** Share your financial experiences and beliefs to create a safe space for open dialogue. This vulnerability can encourage your partner to reciprocate and share their thoughts and concerns.
- **Take It Slow:** Don't overwhelm your partner with a barrage of questions all at once. Start with more straightforward, general inquiries and gradually delve deeper as your comfort level grows.
- **Be Respectful:** Respect your partner's boundaries and avoid pressuring them to disclose more than they're comfortable with. If they seem hesitant to discuss specific topics, give them time and space and revisit the conversation later.
- **Focus on the Future:** Frame the discussion around planning for your future together rather than dwelling on past financial mistakes or differences. This forward-thinking approach can help keep the conversation constructive and optimistic.
- **Stress Teamwork:** Stress that these conversations are about laying a solid financial foundation together. Let your partner know you are committed to working together to build a strong financial foundation, reach your goals, and tackle any challenges that come your way.

MANAGING FINANCES TOGETHER

Now that you've settled into your relationship and had the initial money talk where you found perfect alignment in your money personalities, congratulations! But don't think your job is done. Just as we regularly service our cars, maintaining open communication about money as a couple is super important for keeping your financial relationship strong and healthy.

Set Aside Regular Time for Money Talks: Make money conversations a regular part of your relationship by scheduling dedicated time to discuss your finances. This could be a weekly or monthly check-in where you review your budget, track your progress toward goals, and address any concerns or challenges.

Create Joint Budgets: Creating and sticking to a joint budget is crucial for financial harmony. Both partners must commit to the plan to avoid frustration and mistrust. While occasional slip-ups are normal, frequent deviations from the budget can lead to serious issues. We'll delve deeper into budgeting in a later chapter, so keep an eye out for that critical topic.

Joint Bank Accounts: Wondering if a joint bank account with your spouse is a good idea? It depends on your situation. In the banking chapter, you'll see that syncing your accounts with your budget is an excellent way to keep money organised and easy to manage.

For example, if you both know your monthly expenses like utilities, rent, and mortgage, a joint account can handle these. Each partner keeps their own account for income but transfers money to the joint account for shared bills. This way, you both manage household costs while keeping your financial independence.

The Impact of Credit Scores: If one partner has bad credit and the other has good credit, opening a joint account can hurt the person with good credit. A joint account connects both credit histories, so it's better to avoid joint accounts.

Being honest about your credit history is key. Before opening a joint bank, make sure you both understand each other's credit situation.

To wrap up, money compatibility is super important in relationships. Start talking about finances early, ideally before big commitments like marriage or having kids. Keep the conversation going and work together on money matters for a healthy partnership.

CHAPTER SEVEN—CORE LESSONS

- Choosing a life partner is the most crucial financial decision, highlighting the importance of selecting a financially compatible partner.
- Financial compatibility is essential for the longevity of a relationship, emphasising the need for alignment in money values and goals.
- Money mindsets, influenced by upbringing and experiences, can evolve positively over time.
- Patriarchy in African and Black communities can complicate aligning differing money mindsets, particularly affecting women.
- Financial compatibility can mitigate the harmful effects of patriarchy on Black and African women, offering a pathway to financial empowerment.
- Observing spending habits can provide valuable insights into a partner's financial behaviour.
- Asking questions centred around fundamental financial principles can facilitate productive discussions about money.
- Timing is crucial for financial discussions, ensuring both partners are receptive and engaged.
- Framing discussions positively and maintaining respect fosters open communication and collaboration.
- Emphasising teamwork and focusing on the future encourages joint financial planning and decision-making efforts.
- Regular and ongoing money talks are vital for maintaining financial transparency and alignment in a relationship.

- Joint budgets and bank accounts require commitment and honesty to promote financial accountability and trust.
- Credit scores impact joint accounts and should be openly discussed to make informed financial decisions.

Chapter Seven—Exercise

If Single and Not Yet in a Committed Relationship—Financial Vision Board

Create a visual representation of your financial goals by assembling a vision board with images or words depicting your aspirations, such as a dream house or quotes about financial freedom. Display the board prominently to remind you of your objectives and values.

Purpose

- Articulate your financial aspirations and priorities clearly, providing clarity for future decision-making.
- Gain a deeper understanding of your values and attitudes toward money management.
- Use the vision board to assess alignment with potential life partners, initiating constructive conversations about financial compatibility.
- Identify potential red flags in financial compatibility and lay the groundwork for future financial planning efforts with a compatible partner.

If Already in a Committed Relationship and Money Is a Source of Conflict—Financial Values Discussion

Set aside dedicated time to openly discuss individual financial values and beliefs with your partner. Alternate sharing how upbringing has influenced your money mindset and express any financial goals you have. Practice active listening and respect without judgment.

Purpose

- Deepen understanding of each other's values, beliefs, and money-related goals.
- Improve communication and create a safe space for discussing sensitive financial topics within the relationship.
- Work toward alignment of financial goals, aspirations, and priorities, fostering unity and shared vision.
- Enhance conflict resolution skills by navigating differences in financial values and finding compromises. Strengthen emotional connection by sharing vulnerable aspects of financial upbringing and aspirations.
- Collaborate on future financial planning efforts based on shared understanding and mutual respect.

Chapter Eight

BUDGETING YOUR WAY TO FINANCIAL GREATNESS

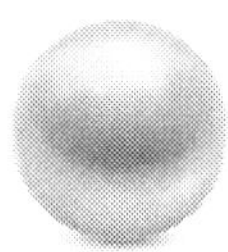

This chapter is absolutely crucial—the queen of all chapters! By reading, absorbing, and applying the strategies discussed here, you're setting yourself up to build lasting wealth. Wealth that you can pass down to future generations. Wealth that can help you surpass the average wealth for a Black family—currently around £34,000 compared to the UK average of £286,000.

Building wealth requires capital—whether you call it savings, investment funds, start-up costs, or seed money. This capital must come from somewhere. And, unless you're one of the lucky few with a wealthy benefactor willing to fund your wealth-building activities, this capital will have to come from your current income. But here's the problem: many of us struggle just to keep up with day-to-day expenses, let alone set money aside for wealth-building.

That's where a budget comes in. A well-crafted budget is your blueprint for managing your finances and allocating your income to help achieve your financial goals. It goes beyond simply tracking what comes in and what goes out; A budget helps you make intentional decisions to prioritise your financial goals and ensure that your wealth-building money emerges victorious in the battle against daily expenses.

Most of us prioritise paying essential bills because the consequences of not doing so are immediate. Miss your mortgage payment, and you risk losing your home. Not paying your rent can render you homeless. Unpaid utilities mean no electricity, gas, water, or Wi-Fi. We pay these bills because we can't afford the inconvenience of neglecting them. But what about the expenses that aren't essential? Saving money is a good financial habit, but it's not a bill that demands payment. Investing builds wealth, but no one forces you to invest. As a result, these non-essential yet crucial financial habits often get overlooked. Many people intend to save, but they first focus on the essentials and plan to save whatever is left. This book is about building wealth, and I assume you want to build wealth. To build wealth, you must take a hard look at your spending habits and reorder your priorities. Freeing up money for wealth-building requires intentional choices and a commitment to making saving and investing as important as paying your essential bills. This means identifying and cutting back on unnecessary expenses—those daily or monthly indulgences that might bring short-term satisfaction but don't contribute to your long-term financial health. These could include frequent dining out, unused subscriptions, or impulsive shopping. While these expenses may seem small on their own, they add up quickly and can divert funds away from your wealth-building efforts.

As a former mortgage adviser, I saw firsthand how this plays out. We'd ask applicants to list all their expenses; shockingly, 90% couldn't account for all their income. They'd have unexplained amounts missing, averaging £250 monthly. Over ten years, that's £30,000! Imagine what you could do with that money if you kept track of it and put it into savings, investments, or even a business. The growth potential is staggering.

If building wealth is your financial goal, then cutting down on non-essential expenses has to be your priority. Every penny saved from trimming these costs is a penny that can be invested in your future. This doesn't mean you have to live a life of austerity, but it does mean being intentional about where your money goes.

ROCK, PEBBLE & SAND

To visualise your budget, consider it a game of *Rock, Pebble, and Sand.* This simple analogy teaches us about prioritising and what happens when we don't prioritise in the correct order.

Imagine a jar representing your entire monthly income in front of you. Next to it are three types of items: large rocks, smaller pebbles, and fine grains of sand. The goal is to fit everything into the jar without leaving anything out.

Most people start by pouring in the sand. Then, they add the rocks. The rocks manage to fit, but there's no room left for the pebbles.

What if I told you that the rocks represent your essential bills, the pebbles—your wealth-building activities and the sand—your fun and discretionary spending?

This analogy describes what happens with most people's money: Essential bills and fun take priority over wealth-building activities.

Here's the trick to fit everything in the jar: start with the rocks—your essential bills. They fit snugly at the bottom of the jar. Next, add the pebbles—your wealth-building activities. They slide into the spaces around the rocks. Finally, pour in the sand—your fun and discretionary spending. It trickles into the gaps left by the rocks and pebbles. When done in this order, everything fits perfectly.

THE 50/30/20 RULE

The 50/30/20 rule is a popular budgeting strategy that suggests allocating your net income as follows: 50% for essentials, 30% for discretionary spending, and 20% for wealth-building activities.

Aim to keep essentials such as housing, utilities, and groceries to 50% of your income. Always look for ways to reduce these expenses, like lowering mortgage payments, finding cheaper insurance, or cutting utility bills. Saving money here frees up funds for other priorities.

Next, dedicate 20% of your income to wealth-building activities, like creating an emergency fund, paying off debt, saving for retirement, and investing. This category often gets overlooked, so you need to be intentional. Don't think, "I'll save whatever is left after paying my bills." The truth is, nothing will be left unless you set it aside first. Make saving a priority, not an afterthought. Have a line dedicated to this category in your budget. And if you can save more than 20%, do it!

The rule allows 30% for fun and discretionary spending—things like dining out, entertainment, and non-essential shopping. I'm not here to spoil your fun—we should absolutely enjoy our money. But it's easy to overspend here, which detracts from what you should invest in your "pebbles." Remember, those pebbles are key to building wealth and achieving financial goals. While fun money is important, it should come after your bigger priorities. Personally, I've always thought 30% for fun is high, but how much you allocate depends on your goals and where you are on your financial journey.

There are many budgeting strategies, but don't get too bogged down by spending rules. Make your own rules that align with your financial goals. Remember, if you prioritise correctly—rocks first, pebbles second, and sand last—you'll meet your big priorities and achieve your financial goals without sacrificing the fun.

MY INCOME IS IRREGULAR

Irregular income can make budgeting tricky, but there are solutions. Let's think back to an old story—the tale of Joseph in ancient Egypt. Joseph predicted there would be seven years of good harvests, followed by seven years of famine. A bit of forward planning and aggressive saving was the solution then, and I dare say that solution will work for you today.

Some of us experience irregular income—some months, we earn more, while in others, our income is lower or even non-existent. That's where a multiple-month budget comes in handy.

When our income is higher in the good months, we can save aggressively for the lean months. This helps us avoid surprises like unexpected expenses or times when we don't earn as much.

So, it's essential to plan your budget in advance. Try to plan at least three months ahead, but ideally, aim for six to twelve months. Let's look at Mary as an example. Mary is a new entrepreneur offering consulting services. Unlike when she was employed and had a steady monthly salary, her income now comes from clients who sometimes pay late.

Here's what Mary does:

1. Mary prepares her budget. She knows exactly how much she spends each month, even though her income varies.
2. Mary uses a spreadsheet to plan her budget for the next 6 to 12 months. A multi-month budget planner helps Mary anticipate cash flow fluctuations and plan accordingly. This enhanced visibility reduces the risk of overspending or being caught off guard by unexpected expenses.
3. Let's say Mary earns £8,000 in January. She knows she might not receive much money from her clients until April. So, she

uses £6,000 out of the £8,000 to cover expenses from January to March and saves the extra £2,000 for when no income is received.

Using a spreadsheet to manage your money has an advantage over most budget apps because you can create a multi-month budget. Most apps show your monthly budget, which is great for tracking your money in the present. However, if you have irregular income or one-off expenses, a budget that looks many months ahead is more helpful.

Below is an example of what a multi-month budget looks like. The great thing about this type of budget is that you only need to fill it in once and then adjust it as each month approaches.

Category	Jan	Feb	Mar	April	Expense Category
Income	£3,630	£3,630	£3,630	£3,630	
Rent/Mortgage	£1,115	£1,115	£1,115	£1,115	
Utilities	£150	£150	£150	£150	**Essentials**
Groceries	£350	£350	£350	£350	
Transportation	£100	£100	£100	£100	
Insurance	£100	£100	£100	£100	
Emergency Fund	£500	£500	£500	£500	
Debt Repayment	£300	£300	£300	£300	
Investment	£200	£200	£200	£200	**Financial Goals**
Retirement Savings	£400	£400	£400	£400	
Misc Savings	£215	£215	£215	£215	
Fun Money	£200	£200	£200	£200	**Wants**

If you need a ready-made template with a multi-month spreadsheet, head over to the Simple Money Hacks website: www.simplemoneyhacks.com. You'll find this sheet on the resource page. It's free, and you don't need to buy any special software since it's a Google Sheet.

Mary can use a similar budget template to plan ahead and be proactive with her budget. By doing so, she can navigate the ups and downs of irregular income more effectively.

I HAVE MORE EXPENSES THAN INCOME—WHAT DO I DO?

The 50/30/20 budget strategy is fine and dandy when there is enough income to cover your essentials, financial goals, and wants. But what happens if you start your budget and find that you don't have enough money to cover all categories? Say you only have enough to cover the essentials. It's not the worst position, but it means you are working just to pay bills, with nothing set aside for the future and nothing to spark joy in the present. The worst position to be in is not having enough to cover even the basics. Now, if your budget has revealed that you are exceeding your income, don't panic. You are not alone here. This is where most people find themselves at the start of fixing their finances. With a few nips and tucks, you will soon be on your way to financial recovery. But you need to do the following:

1. Acknowledging the severity of the situation—that's just what it is. Face the daunting reality head-on, accept that change is necessary, and muster the courage to take action.
2. Next comes the daunting task of budget construction. Gather your payslips and bank statements. Crank open your banking app. You will need these to construct a realistic budget. Your income and every expense, big or small, should be on your list. The aim is to see everything written plainly.
3. What are the expenses you can do without? You can't have everything you want. You need to choose what expense stays and what goes. Some things may need to be set aside for now and revisited later when your finances improve. Take a close look at your expenses, sifting through each category to identify areas where you can cut back. Are there unnecessary costs that can be reduced or eliminated entirely? Can you renegotiate utility bills or find cheaper alternatives to ease the financial burden?

My Story: I began budgeting when my finances were in complete chaos—my basic expenses alone were swallowing more than my entire income. There wasn't a penny left for savings, let alone fun. That's when I stumbled upon the 50/30/20 budget rule. My essentials gobbled up 105% of my income, plunging me deeper into debt. It was a miserable existence. But, once I learned about the 50/30/20 budget, turning a blind eye to my finances was no longer an option. The thought of sinking further into debt each month was unsettling. Slashing my essential expenses from 105% to 50% seemed impossible—how could I possibly cut my costs by over half? I felt fear and was tempted to just ignore the problem. But I knew it would only get worse. So, I did exactly what I am now asking you to do.

With the help of my payslips and bank statements, I made a good ol' fashioned paper and pen budget. With surgical precision, I cut out expenses that I deemed unnecessary for my survival. To make my decision stick, I actually wrote out the expenses I cut and stuck them on my mirror as a daily reminder.

- Thou shall pack lunch to work.
- Thou shall no longer buy lunch at work.
- Thou shall sell thy car and find cheaper ways to travel.
- Thou shall not upgrade thy phone contract and stick with thy Nokia 3310 for the foreseeable future.

No, I did not need to write my decision in dramatic, old-fashioned English, but it made me laugh, and I needed a source of joy during this painful transition.

These simple actions trimmed 10% off my expenses. Yay! At least my expenses no longer exceeded my income.

Trimming expenses is an important first step. By trimming your expenses, you are fixing money the leaks. There is no point in going after more money just to leak it all away. But there is only so much cost-cutting a person can do. Once you cut out every unnecessary expense, the next action is to increase your income.

I slept on the living room floor for 18 months while renting my room to a lodger. In addition, I got a raise from my employer. Cutting expenses and increasing income meant I could pay off debts, further lowering my expenses and eventually allowing me to save and invest.

CREATING YOUR OWN BUDGET

Managing money with a budget for the first time can seem overwhelming for many. We often view budgets as restrictive, time-consuming joy suckers, but as we become accustomed to budgeting, we soon discover that instead of sucking the life out of us, budgets give our finances a new lease on life.

Think of a budget as a simple to-do list for your finances. Women, in particular, enjoy to-do lists—I know I do. A budget is essentially a "to-pay" list.

Approach your budget as a straightforward list: list your income and your expenses, and then subtract your expenses from your income. This uncomplicated method makes budgeting more approachable and less intimidating. When we don't keep track of our finances, it often leads to underlying worries that weigh heavily on our minds, whether we consciously acknowledge them or not. A written budget takes the worry from your mind, helps you visualise where your money is going, and provides a clear plan to reverse negative trends.

Zero-Based Budget

A zero-based budget (ZBB) is about giving every pound you earn a purpose so that your income matches your expenses. This means you assign your income to your expenses, financial goals, and threats, leaving a zero balance with no money unallocated.

I get a few raised eyebrows every time I mention this budget type to clients. *"You mean I should spend every penny with nothing left over?"* they ask. That's not it at all. Don't live hand to mouth; instead, plan all your expenses, including savings and money for fun, within your budget.

Have a look at the example below:

Income	**£3,630**
Essentials	£1,815
Financial Goals	£1,615
Fun and Discretionary Spending	£200
Total Expenses	£3,630
Total Income	£3,630
Left Overs	£0.00

At the beginning of budgeting, you might focus more on paying off high-interest debt rather than saving or investing. If the interest on your debts is higher than what you'd earn from saving, it makes sense to prioritise debt repayment. Still, have a dedicated line in your budget for debt repayment. Once you clear your debts, pay what you once paid for debt repayment for saving instead.

Make room in your budget for treats and fun stuff. Spending feels great and guilt-free when you plan fun money spending ahead of time. Furthermore, planning fun money spending might help you focus on fun activities that generate lasting memories rather than random, forgettable items.

Managing your money with a budget gets easier over time. At first, money might feel tight, like being stuck in a traffic jam with little room to move while you are rushing to get to your destination. But if you stick with it and stay disciplined, the traffic starts to clear, and you can move freely. Eventually, you'll have more money to do what you want. Just be ready to put in the effort and discipline at the beginning.

Budget Formats

Using pen and paper is an easy and accessible way to begin budgeting, especially if you're used to detailing your income and expenses weekly or monthly. The pen-and-paper method allows you to get started immediately.

Alternatively, spreadsheets offer a more efficient approach, as you don't have to repeatedly list your income and expenses. Since these figures tend to remain pretty consistent from month to month, using a spreadsheet allows you to simply replicate your previous entries and make adjustments for any new or occasional income and expenses. All you need is a computer or smartphone. Google Sheets is free and has everything you need. Learning to use spreadsheets may take a few minutes to familiarise yourself if you're new to them, but the benefits are well worth it.

If you prefer the convenience of technology, various budgeting apps are available for download on your phone. These apps offer several advantages, such as automatically linking to your bank account to retrieve income and expense information, eliminating the need for manual input. This feature is beneficial for busy individuals, as it provides real-time updates on your spending compared to your budget.

Expense tracking becomes effortless with budgeting apps, as transactions are automatically categorised and detailed reports are generated to monitor your spending within your predetermined categories. Best of all, once downloaded, these apps are always at your fingertips, allowing you to check your budget anytime and anywhere.

Practice Makes Perfect

Cut yourself some slack as you begin this budgeting journey. It's normal to stumble along the way, so don't be too hard on yourself if things don't go perfectly initially. You might still spend more than you planned in certain areas. This could mean that you didn't allocate enough money to start with. Simply adjust your budget by allocating more funds where needed. Or it could be that old overspending habits die hard; commit to reining in spending and be more disciplined in the future. Don't give up. If you genuinely want to improve, you'll get there eventually.

Seeing the numbers shift in your favour is rewarding. Evolving from barely having enough money to cover expenses to having money left over sparks joy. Keeping essential expenses below 50% and directing the extra toward your financial goals gets you closer to the dream of financial peace and builds your confidence.

If you have out-of-control, high-interest consumer debt, a budget will help you focus on paying off debts.

Mental budgets don't work. Try to remember everything you spent your money on last month. You'll likely find that you can't recall where all your money went—and we're not just talking about small pennies here, but significant amounts that seem to vanish without explanation. A carefully planned budget helps eliminate this mystery and ensures that all your money goes where you want it to.

Consider this: Even mega-rich companies like Amazon, Apple, and Coca-Cola rely on budgets to handle their finances wisely. If budgets are essential for them, they're vital for you and me. The less money we have, the more we need a budget to monitor our limited funds to eliminate waste.

Allocating Your Income

Let's break down budget allocation using a simple example with Mary. Mary earns a take-home pay of £2,400 per month.

Using the 50/30/20 here, budget allocations work out as follows:

Essentials Expenses	£3,630 x 50% = £1,815
Financial Goals Fund	£3,630 x 20% = £726
Fun & Discretionary Spending	£3,630 x 30% = £1,089

Remember that the 50/30/20 rule is just a guideline; adjust it to fit your needs.

Here's how to work out your budget backwards:

You already know what you spend your money on each month. Maybe you just want to see how much you spend in each category. It's super easy to figure out.

1. **Categorise Your Spending**: Start by sorting your expenses into three categories: Essentials, fun & discretionary spending, and financial Goals.
2. **Tally Up Each Category**: Add the total amount you spend in each category. This will give you a clear picture of where your money is going each month.
3. **Do the Math**:

Monthly Take-Home Pay	£3,630
Monthly Essentials Bills	£1,815

Divide the total spending on essentials by your monthly salary, then multiply by 100, like so: £1,815 / £3,630 x 100 = 50%

Now it's your turn! Calculate the proportions of your income allocated to essentials, fun and discretionary spending, and financial goals. This exercise will help you understand where your money is going and if any adjustments are needed to better align with your financial priorities.

CHAPTER EIGHT—CORE LESSONS

- Budgeting helps you manage your money and work toward your financial goals, whether saving for a home, paying off debt, or building wealth for retirement.
- By tracking your income and expenses, a budget allows you to identify areas where you may be overspending or wasting money. This awareness empowers you to make adjustments and allocate your resources more effectively, ensuring that every pound you earn is put to good use.
- With limited resources, it's essential to prioritise spending. A budget helps you distinguish between needs and fun money, ensuring that you allocate your money to essentials and financial goals before discretionary purchases.
- Budgeting becomes even more critical if you struggle to make ends meet or face unpredictable income fluctuations. It provides structure and discipline to your finances, helping you navigate challenging financial circumstances.
- One fundamental principle of budgeting is to pay yourself first. This means allocating a portion of your income toward savings, investments, and debt repayment before allocating funds to discretionary expenses. By prioritising these financial goals, you lay the foundation for long-term financial stability and growth.
- While budgeting frameworks such as the 50/30/20 rule can provide a helpful starting point, it's essential to tailor your budget to your unique financial circumstances and goals. Feel free to adjust these proportions based on your priorities and objectives.

- Like any new habit, budgeting requires consistency and perseverance. While it may feel challenging or overwhelming initially, stick with it, and you'll gradually become more comfortable and confident in managing your finances. Over time, budgeting will become second nature.

Chapter Eight—Exercise

1. **Create Your Budget:** Start by listing all your income sources and expenses. If your expenses exceed your income, identify areas where you can cut back to bring your spending in line with your earnings.
2. **Explore Income-Boosting Opportunities:** Consider ways to increase your income using resources unique to you. This could involve pursuing freelance work, starting a side hustle, or leveraging your skills for additional income streams.
3. **Allocate Funds to Financial Goals:** Prioritise your financial goals, whether it's building an emergency fund, paying off high-interest debt, or saving for a specific milestone. Allocate a portion of your income toward these goals to make steady progress over time.
4. **Incorporate Fun Money:** It's important to include some fun money in your budget for leisure activities and enjoyment. Determine an amount that aligns with your current financial situation and future aspirations, ensuring it doesn't compromise your other financial objectives.

You have various options to initiate your budgeting journey:

- **Traditional Method:** Start with pen and paper to manually track your income and expenses.
- **Mobile Budgeting App:** Use a user-friendly budgeting app on your smartphone for convenient tracking and management.

- **Simple Spreadsheet:** Download a straightforward budget spreadsheet from the resources page at www.simplemoneyhacks.com. This tool provides a structured format to organise your finances effectively.

Chapter Nine

ORGANISED BANKING FOR SEAMLESS PERSONAL FINANCE MANAGEMENT

Let's do a quick recap, shall we? You now understand the absolute importance of managing your money through budgets. You're aware of your essential needs and financial goals, and let's not forget the treats for a bit of jollification. I am all for striking that balance in life—work hard, play hard (within reason and budget, of course).

The way we organise our banking can make gaining control of our finances challenging. Life is busy, and keeping track of money might feel like yet another task on an already long to-do list. To keep things easy and in line, we should set up our banking in the same way we've set up our budget—separating essential bills, fun spending, and financial goal commitments.

The beauty of gaining control over our finances lies in setting up an automatic system where bills are paid, savings are made, and spending is managed without spending hours organising it. Once set up, you won't need to dedicate too much time each month—just 15 minutes should suffice.

Let's use Tera as our example. Tera set up her budget, knowing exactly how much she needed for essentials, savings, and treats. Her main bank account, where her salary is paid, serves as the central hub for her financial activities. She uses it to receive income, pay bills, make daily purchases, and manage savings.

Despite categorising her budget into essentials, fun money, and financial goals, Tera found it challenging to keep track of everyday expenses, bills, and savings. By mid-month, she often lost sight of what has been paid, pending direct debits, and upcoming subscription payments.

After a particularly tough week at work, Tera treats herself to a delicious double chocolate chip cupcake. She reckoned she had at least £10 left in her bank account—the cupcake was only £3. However, this tiny purchase led to a chain reaction of financial woes. A few days later, she received a notification of a failed direct debit due to insufficient funds in her account, triggering a hefty penalty fee of £25. That £3 cupcake splurge left Tera with only £7 remaining in her account. Unfortunately, she had overlooked an upcoming payment of £8 scheduled for the next day.

Banks, huh? Luckily, Tera got the charge waived by her bank after some persuasion, but her bank warned that future missed direct debits wouldn't be forgiven.

Tera's struggle isn't unique. Many of us find keeping tabs on bank transactions a challenge, especially with our busy schedules. Who has time to scrutinise bank statements daily? It's easy to lose track of payments, due dates, and available funds.

CHALLENGE BANK FEES

I vividly recall an incident when a client walked into my bank branch. She had been hit with four bank charges for missing four direct debit payments, amounting to £100. Already struggling to keep up with her bills, she was fortunate to have all the fees waived on that occasion. And here's my first tip: whenever your bank slaps you with a fee, don't hesitate to challenge it. Whether it's your first fee or your hundredth, speak up.

Ramit Sethi provides a helpful script for negotiating with your bank to waive fees in his book "*I Will Teach You To Be Rich*". The key points are: remain polite, avoid asking yes-or-no questions, and don't give up if the bank representative is being difficult. Clearly state your objective of having the fees waived. If these charges are unusual for you, mention that (Sethi, 2009). If frequent charges are an issue, explain that you're actively working to improve your finances, and waiving this fee will support your efforts. Politely insist on their assistance in getting your finances on track.

If calling your bank makes you uncomfortable, especially if you get charged quite often, still make the call. Feeling discomfort has its reward. I remember this feeling and how it made me more determined never to get charged again.

REVISIT YOUR BUDGET

People don't miss bill payments on purpose. Usually, it's because they're short on funds or an oversight, as in the case of Tera. If this is the case, revisit your budget and find areas to cut back on. The last thing you want when already grappling with bills is to incur extra charges.

Many of us rely on one main bank account for everything—from receiving our salaries to paying bills and shopping. It's easy to forget about pending payments, especially nearing month's end. A forgotten pending card transaction can push us into unauthorised overdrafts and attract bank charges.

What compounds this issue is that, aside from the bank's charge for a missed direct debit and the unauthorised overdraft fee, the company you failed to pay due to the bounced payment can also impose charges. For instance, if you miss your gas bill due to insufficient funds, your bank and the gas company can penalise you. Furthermore, missed payments on your bank account can adversely affect your credit score—ouch! Our goal should be to prevent missed payments proactively to avoid these repercussions.

SEPARATE YOUR ACCOUNTS

One proactive approach to avoiding missing payments is to rethink how we manage our bank accounts. Why have one bank account to manage our salaries and other payment transactions? These payments are often spread out across different days of the month, some falling perilously close to the month's end when funds may be tight.

Instead of relying solely on one account for all transactions, why not consider opening a separate bank account specifically for bill payments? There's no rule dictating that we must have only one bank account. This secondary account needn't be fancy. The essential requirement is that it allows for direct debits, standing orders, and card payments, ideally with a Visa or Mastercard facility.

By establishing an account dedicated to bill payments, you can simply transfer the total amount of your monthly bills into the new bill account. Don't shop with your bill account, so there's no risk of inadvertently spending bill money. With your bill money separated, your main account should primarily hold funds for groceries and discretionary spending.

This system works best when combined with your budget. Your budget should outline your monthly bills and any expected increases and guide how much you transfer to your bill account.

Tera read this book and has now reorganised her banking to align with her budget.

Here's how Tera restructured her banking:

Step 1: Tera opened a new bank account specifically for paying bills.

Step 2: She contacted all her utility and bill providers to inform them of her new payment account and provided them with the new account details.

Step 3: Tera requested that her direct debits be scheduled for collection after she receives her salary.

Step 4: Since Tera gets paid on the 28th of each month, she set her payments to be deducted on the 1st of the following month, allowing 3-4 days to manage her finances.

Step 5: Tera continues to have her salary deposited into her longstanding main bank account.

Step 6: With her monthly bills totalling £1,800, she transfers this amount into her new bills account each month.

Step 7: All bills are paid from this new account, which Tera keeps separate from her spending, ensuring there's always enough to cover her bills, regardless of their due dates.

Once the transfers are made, any leftover funds in Tera's main account are for grocery and discretionary spending. She can enjoy her indulgences guilt-free, knowing her finances are in order. She no longer spends hours managing her money and easily sticks to her budget for saving and spending. This simple setup ensures financial goals are met, bills are paid on time, and guilt-free spending is always possible.

ALTERNATIVE STRATEGY

Alternatively, Tera could open a new account for her discretionary and grocery shopping. She would keep bill payments in her main bank account and transfer spending money to the new one. This avoids the hassle of updating utility providers with new bank details. Tera would only use her longstanding main bank account for bills and her new account for spending. Additionally, Tera has set up savings and investment accounts, to which she transfers predetermined amounts—again, in line with her budget.

THE BEST BANK ACCOUNTS

There are various bank account options suitable for your bill account needs. You can simply approach your current bank and request to set up a second account. You can do this online. Remember, this account doesn't need to be fancy—it just needs to allow money transfers and bill payments.

Digital banks offer a convenient alternative, often with softer credit checks, making them accessible to many in the UK. I like the newer digital banks like Monzo, Starling, Wise, Revolut, and Tide. They're incredibly user-friendly, with easy account setup and real-time transaction notifications. Plus, they provide all the necessary features, including direct debit, standing order, and card payment facilities.

To sum things up, here are four straightforward steps:

1. **Open a dedicated bank account for your bills.** Start by opening a separate account solely for paying bills, such as rent, mobile phone charges, or utility bills. You can ask your current bank for a basic account with direct debit and standing order capabilities or explore options with online banks like Monzo, Starling, or Revolut, which are incredibly user-friendly.
2. **Add all your bills to this new account.** Provide your utilities and bill companies with the details of your new bill account, including a sort code (a six-digit number, e.g., 01-02-03) and an account number (an eight-digit number). You can do this conveniently online or by calling the billing company.
3. **Transfer enough money to cover your bills.** Ensure you transfer sufficient funds into the new account each month. You can manually do this or set up an automatic transfer from your main account.
4. **Keep an eye on your new setup.** Monitor your bill payments when transferring from your old account to the new bill account to ensure the transfer is complete.

In addition to automating bill payments, leverage the technological advancements banks offer to optimise your banking experience. Here's how it works:

SUPERCHARGE YOUR FINANCES WITH TECHNOLOGY

1. **Get Helpful Alerts:** Your bank can notify you of upcoming bills, unusual payments, and low balances.
2. **Stay on Top of Your Finances:** Alerts help prevent missed payments and detect suspicious activity.

3. **Mobile Banking Convenience:** Mobile apps let you handle everything from setting up transfers to cancelling direct debits, all at your fingertips.
4. **Budgeting Tools:** Online banks like Monzo and Starling offer intuitive tools to simplify budgeting and expense tracking and keep you in control.

By embracing organised banking, you're taking control of your financial destiny. With strategic budgeting, account separation, and leveraging technology, you'll streamline bill payments, boost savings, and eliminate financial stress. So, take charge, stay organised, and watch your financial goals become a reality. Organised banking isn't just a method—it's a game-changer!

CHAPTER NINE—CORE LESSONS

- Aligning your budget with your banking is crucial for managing personal finances effectively.
- Using separate bank accounts for different purposes, such as bills, savings, and discretionary spending, helps avoid overspending and missed payments.
- Digital banks like Monzo, Starling, and Revolut work well as bill accounts and offer user-friendly features, including budgeting tools and easy account setup.
- Leveraging technology, including mobile and online banking tools, enhances financial control and convenience.
- Banking alerts help monitor account activity, detect unusual transactions, and ensure sufficient funds.
- Regularly review your bills to ensure you're transferring the correct amounts and avoid missed payments.

Chapter Nine—Exercise

If you find yourself missing direct debit payments or simply want to get more organised with your banking, follow these steps:

1. **Create a Budget:** Organise your finances with a budget to determine the total amount of your monthly bills.
2. **Open a Dedicated Bill Payment Account:** Establish a separate bank account exclusively for bill payments.
3. **Automate Transfers:** Arrange automatic transfers from your main account to the dedicated bill payment account.
4. **Ensure Sufficient Funds:** Verify that the transferred amount covers all your monthly bills.
5. **Notify Utility Suppliers:** Inform all your utility suppliers to deduct payments from the dedicated bill payment account.
6. **Monthly Recurrence:** Let the process repeat automatically every month.
7. **Bank Alerts:** Set up banking alerts to notify you of low balances or higher-than-normal payments.
8. **Review:** Compare your actual spending to your budget at the end of the month and adjust as needed.

Chapter Ten

UNDERSTANDING CREDIT

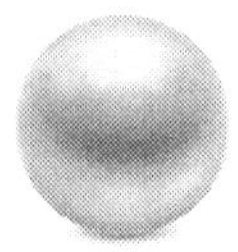

Credit is the ever-intimidating, invisible concept that dictates our financial lives. Don't worry if the word credit makes you cringe; in this chapter, we'll dive into understanding credit, its uses, and how to use it wisely. Many finance books demonise credit and debt, but credit can boost our financial freedom if used correctly.

I once read a popular finance book that denounced all borrowing, including mortgages, and suggested that people should save up hundreds of thousands of pounds to buy a home in cash, which seemed like impractical advice to me. I don't know many people with £500,000 saved up to buy a home outright.

This approach is actually detrimental; building credit early on is important to get approved for items like mortgages; some landlords even check credit before approving a rental application—it ensures they can trust you, as your credit history shows your ability to pay your rent on time. So, although having debt feels counterintuitive if it's handled responsibly, it sets you up for an easier journey.

A better approach is understanding credit and knowing how to use credit wisely. In this chapter, I'll share my experiences to help you make better decisions so you can get the most out of using credit. If you've made mistakes with your credit, I hope what I share will help you fix them.

WHAT IS CREDIT?

Credit means debt—it's borrowing cash and committing to pay it back down the line. It allows you to buy stuff even if you don't have the money now. Getting a mortgage to buy your dream home or using overdrafts, credit cards, store cards, and various types of loans are all forms of credit.

With credit comes credit agreements. Credit agreements are documents packed with terms and conditions, often known as T&Cs. These are simply the rules you've got to stick to in order to keep things sweet with the lender. Within these T&Cs is the borrowed amount, called the principal, and the interest rate—that's the percentage fee for borrowing cash.

With some agreements, you find a repayment schedule laying out how much you owe each time (usually every month) and when it's due. If you have ever wondered how many payments it takes to clear that loan, it's usually in the agreement. Plus, it breaks down each payment to show what you are paying back toward what you borrowed (the principal) and what you are paying for the interest.

Extra fees or charges also show up in the agreement. The T&Cs might hold even more info, so it's good to read it before signing on that dotted line.

Credit File

A credit file is like a report card for your money habits. It keeps track of things like loans and credit cards and how good you are at paying bills on time. Think of it as a record that shows how trustworthy you are with money. Banks and utility companies use it to decide if they want to lend you money or provide services like phone contracts. So, it's pretty important to keep it in good shape. If you ask to borrow money or apply for services like a phone contract or utilities and get denied, it still gets recorded on your credit file. This means lenders and service providers can see how often you're asking for credit, even if you don't get approved. Too many requests for credit in a short time can make you look desperate to borrow, which isn't great for your credit score. Multiple rejections within a short period, like three to six months, can signal to lenders that you might be having financial difficulties or struggling to manage your money. So, it's wise to be strategic about how often you apply for credit to maintain a healthy credit profile.

WHO IS WATCHING YOU?

In the UK, there are at least three agencies that keep tabs on your credit activities: Experian, Equifax, and TransUnion. These agencies gather info from banks and lenders. The info they gather includes your personal details, credit accounts, payment history, and any public records (like bankruptcies). All of this data will be logged into your credit file. Your credit file shapes your credit history—which is a record of your credit journey.

Credit Score

All three credit agencies will give you a score based on how you've performed. Here are some key things they consider for a good score:

- **Payment History**: Your track record of paying bills and debts on time.
- **Credit Utilisation**: Credit utilisation refers to the amount of your available credit that you actually use. Take credit cards, for

instance—it's recommended not to go over 30% of your available credit. So, if your credit card offers a £1,000 limit, it's best to stick to spending no more than £300 each month. Then, make sure to pay off this amount in full every month.

- **Length of Credit History**: The length of credit history measures how long your credit accounts have been active. The idea is simple—the longer you've had these credit accounts, the clearer the picture for lenders regarding your financial habits and reliability.
- **Variety of Credit**: Variety in your credit portfolio is more favourable. The idea is this: Having a mix, like a credit card, a loan, an overdraft, and a mortgage, looks better for your credit score than having multiple credit cards alone.
- **Recent Credit Inquiries:** Recent credit inquiries track how frequently you seek new credit. When you make a bunch of credit applications within a short span, let's say three to six months, it might signal to lenders that you're really eager for credit. This eagerness is seen as a sign of financial difficulties. Banks looking out for your financial well-being will hesitate to lend money if they think you're in financial trouble. They also want to ensure they get back any money they lend.

If you regularly pay off your credit card balance and always pay your bills on time, your responsible financial habits get recognised. This recognition leads to excellent credit scores. It's just like the school days: do your homework, pass those tests, and nail those exams for a guaranteed pass at the end of the year.

Just as schools grade with A's, B's, and C's, credit scores are represented by a three-digit number. For instance:

Experian grades from 0 to 999, Equifax offers scores from 0 to 700, and TransUnion assigns numbers from 0 to 710. These numbers are your ticket to understanding how well you're doing in the world of credit. Higher numbers mean better credit scores.

BENEFITS OF A GOOD CREDIT SCORE

Having a good credit score comes with several advantages.

- **Better Loan Approvals***:* An excellent credit score increases your chances of loan approval, giving you access to various borrowing options.
- **Lower Interest Rates***:* With a top-notch credit score, you can secure loans and credit at lower interest rates. This saves you money in the long run by reducing the amount you pay in interest.
- **Higher Credit Limits***:* An excellent credit score can lead to higher credit limits on your cards. This gives you more flexibility and purchasing power when you need it.
- **Easier Rental Approvals***:* Landlords often consider credit scores when reviewing rental applications. With an excellent score, you're more likely to get approved for your dream apartment or house, as it demonstrates financial reliability.
- **Better Insurance Premiums***:* Credit scores can influence insurance premiums. With an excellent credit score, you may qualify for lower rates on insurance policies, such as car or home insurance, as insurers see you as a lower risk.
- **Access to Premium Credit Cards***:* A top-notch credit score opens doors to premium credit card offers with enticing perks like cash-back rewards, travel benefits, and exclusive offers.
- **Enhanced Negotiating Power***:* An excellent credit score gives you more leverage when negotiating financial terms. You can secure lower interest rates on loans or better credit agreement terms, providing greater control over your financial decisions.
- **Improved Job Prospects***:* Some employers, especially in finance-related roles, check credit scores during the hiring process to gauge financial responsibility. A good credit score can give you an edge, showcasing your reliability and trustworthiness.

BUILDING YOUR CREDIT

Building your credit rating is a smart move. Here are some simple tips to help you out:

- **Register on the Electoral Roll**: Register to vote at your current address. It confirms your identity and residence, boosting your credit rating. Check your eligibility at https://www.gov.uk/register-to-vote.
- **Pay Bills on Time**: Pay your bills promptly, including utilities, rent, and mobile phone bills. On-time payments show lenders that you're reliable and responsible.
- **Use a Credit Card Wisely**: Get a credit card and use it responsibly. Start with a low credit limit, make small purchases, and pay off the balance in full each month. Doing so builds a positive credit history. Never put more on your credit cards than you are able to pay off at month's end.
- **Maintain Low Credit Utilisation**: Keep your credit utilisation below 30%. For example, if your credit limit is £1,000, spend no more than £300 monthly. It shows lenders you're responsible with your money and not using all credit available to you.
- **Avoid Missed Payments:** Missing payments harm your credit rating. Set up direct debits or automatic payments to avoid late payments.
- **Avoid Excessive Credit Applications:** Multiple credit applications in a short period raise concerns for lenders.
- **Keep Credit Accounts Open**: If you've managed credit well, consider keeping accounts open. It shows an extended credit history and that you are an experienced credit handler.
- **Check Your Credit Report Regularly**: Monitor your Experian, Equifax, and TransUnion credit reports. Check for accuracy and

report any errors promptly. Regular checks help identify issues and protect against fraud.

Following these tips can help you build a strong credit rating.

Things to Avoid

- **Joint Credit Application with a Person with Bad Credit:** If you apply for credit jointly with someone with bad credit, the application will most likely be rejected. As your name is on the application, it could affect your credit rating negatively. Before applying for joint credit, each party should check their credit report. If there are any blemishes, be wise and don't harm the credit rating that you have worked hard to build. Don't do it, girl. Not even for love!
- **Closing Old Credit Accounts**: Closing old credit accounts can shorten your credit history and potentially lower your credit score. It's generally better to keep them open, especially if they are in good standing.
- **Ignoring Credit Report Errors**: Regularly check your credit report for any errors or discrepancies. If you spot any inaccuracies, report them promptly to the credit reference agencies to have them corrected.
- **Falling for Credit Repair Scams**: Be cautious of companies that promise quick fixes to repair your credit. Many of these companies engage in unethical practices or charge excessive fees. Work on improving your credit through responsible financial behaviour.

Getting Back on Track with Your Credit Score

So, you're reading this chapter and decide to go online to check your credit score. But what you see shocks you—a really low score with the label "poor" right next to it. How did this happen? There could be several reasons. Missed or late payments are common culprits. Sometimes, a low score is due to an error or fraud. But don't panic! Credit scores aren't set in stone; they can improve over time. Here's what you can do to rebuild your credit:

1. Understand your credit situation. Take a look at your credit report. Identify any errors or fraud and ensure they're corrected.
2. If you spot any unpaid bills or defaults on your file, get in touch with the company you owe and try to work out a plan to settle the debt. Over time, these records lose their impact on your file as they age. Making arrangements to pay what you owe can help clear your file and improve your financial standing in the long run.
3. Set up automatic payment systems like direct debits or standing orders for your regular bills to avoid missing payments. Automation reduces human error, such as forgetfulness.
4. Consider applying for a small credit card or a credit-building card designed for those with lower credit scores. Use it wisely by making small purchases and paying off the balance in full each month. This demonstrates responsible credit use and helps rebuild your credit history.
5. Keep your credit utilisation low. I've mentioned this before. But it's really worth repeating: do not max out your credit cards; don't even use half of your credit limit. Aim to use no more than 30% of your limit. Calculating 30% of your limit is straightforward: take the credit card limit provided by your company, multiply it by 30, and then divide by 100. For instance, if your limit stands at £380, 30% would be £380 x 30 / 100 = £114.
6. Make it a habit to settle your credit card bills completely each month. This tip ties back to managing your credit utilisation. When you stick within the 30% limit, repaying the full amount becomes more manageable. If you're genuinely committed to

boosting your credit, aim to never carry over outstanding balances on your credit cards. If you're dealing with a hefty balance already, focus on paying off what you owe and then follow the 30% utilisation rule once your debt is cleared. For those who find it tough to curb overspending, temporarily cutting up the card until you regain control of your finances might be a sensible move.

7. Rebuilding credit takes time and patience. It won't happen overnight, but you can gradually improve your credit rating by consistently following good credit practices. Stay committed, and don't get discouraged along the way.

How Long Do Default, CCJs, and Bankruptcy Stay on Your Credit History?

1. Defaults happen when you miss repayments on a debt.
2. County Court Judgments (CCJs) are legal orders from a UK county court if you've neglected to settle a debt. CCJs can hit your credit score and even lead to legal steps for debt recovery.
3. Bankruptcy: This is a legal process when someone can't pay their debts. It's admitting you can't pay what you owe anymore. Bankruptcy offers a fresh start but comes with serious consequences.

All three stay on your credit history for about six years from the date of the incident. After that, they should vanish from your credit report, and their impact on your credit rating lessens. But remember, it might not happen automatically; keep an eye on your report and reach out to the credit agencies to update your records if needed.

Is it a good idea to pay the defaulted amounts?

Absolutely, it's usually a good call to pay off what you owe if you're able to.

Here's why:

Firstly, it shows lenders that you're taking steps to correct past financial mistakes. While it won't erase the history of defaults, it shows your dedication to meeting financial responsibilities, which can work in your favour and build trust for future credit.

Secondly, settling defaulted debts can help you avoid the hassle of legal actions or die-hard debt collectors. These collectors can make life hell, and paying off debts can help reduce that stress and improve your overall well-being.

Plus, paying off defaults might open up a chance to negotiate with creditors or collection agencies. You could explore options like settling the debt for a lower sum or arranging a payment plan that suits your finances better.

What if You Have No Credit History?

Even if you've never missed paying a bill, you might face credit rejections if you've recently turned 18 or are new to the UK. The challenge lies in having no credit history. Banks and lenders can't see how you've dealt with credit in the past, which leaves them uncertain about how you'll manage credit in the future.

Some people have no credit history because they've been taught that all credit is evil and should be avoided at all costs. This notion is misguided. It's like saying eating food causes weight gain, so to avoid gaining weight, stop eating altogether—absolute nonsense! As with most things in life, handling credit is about finding the right balance.

If you're starting with no credit history, here's how you can quickly build one:

- **Get on the Electoral Roll***:* Make sure you're registered to vote. It helps establish your identity and address.

- **Open a Bank Account***:* Start with a basic current account to manage your money.
- **Start With a Mobile Phone Contract:** Consider getting a contract phone in your name. Regular payments can build a positive credit history.
- **Apply for a Starter Credit Card***:* Look for credit cards designed for newcomers or those with limited credit history. Use it responsibly and pay off the balance in full each month.
- **Use Direct Debits***:* Set up direct debits for regular bills to ensure on-time payments and avoid late fees.
- **Stay Within Credit Limits***:* If you have a credit card, stay within 30% of the available limit. It shows responsible credit usage.
- **Monitor Your Credit***:* Regularly check your credit report to ensure accuracy and spot any issues. Use the free services the three credit reference agencies provide: Experian, Equifax, and TransUnion.
- **Don't Use Credit Repair Companies***:* Be careful when dealing with credit repair companies that promise to fix your credit problems quickly. While some trustworthy companies exist, many may do things that are not right or charge very high fees. It's usually better to focus on improving your credit by being responsible with your money and seeking advice from reliable sources like your bank.
- **Get Educated***:* Learning more about personal finance and credit can give you the knowledge you need to make smarter decisions about your money. Take advantage of resources that can teach you, like workshops or educational materials such as this book. Consider talking to financial advisors who can give you advice that fits your situation.

Remember, building credit takes time, so be patient. By following these steps and being responsible with your finances, you'll be on your way to establishing a positive credit history in the UK.

How Does Your Credit Score Influence Your Borrowing?

Remember our friends from Chapter Six, Ada, Mariam Kayin, and Fatima?

Let's say our ladies want to borrow £15,000 each. This is to illustrate how our money habits impact our credit.

Ada, the investor, is in a good financial position. Her bank account, student loan, and credit card are managed responsibly. She uses a small portion of her available credit, pays it off in full and on time every month, and keeps up with her utility bills. Ada's credit report shows that she has never missed a payment, resulting in an impressive credit score of 940 out of 999. As a result, she receives the loan easily and qualifies for the lowest interest rates.

Mariam, the saver/hoarder, has a straightforward financial setup. She has a bank account where her salary is deposited, as well as a savings account. However, Mariam has never had a credit card and doesn't have bills in her name since she lives with her parents. Her credit report doesn't show much history, except for her voter registration and long-term residency at the same address. As a result, her credit score is average, scoring 780. Despite having substantial savings, she faces limitations in borrowing opportunities. For example, Mariam might qualify for the loan, but her interest rate could be a bit higher. Why? Because she hasn't borrowed much before, the banks aren't sure if she'll pay back on time. You see, it all comes down to credit scores, and computers check these scores. Unlike humans, computers can't reason or appreciate savers like Mariam. They simply focus on your borrowing history. Even though Mariam is good at saving, her lack of borrowing history makes it harder for banks to make a decision.

Kayin, the avoider, has made improvements in managing her finances. She has a bank account, a credit card, and a student loan. Although she had a history of late payments, she has recently started paying her credit card bills on time through a direct debit. Additionally, her roommate, Gina, ensures that all shared bills are paid promptly. These positive changes have improved Kayin's credit score, which now stands at 630. While her score is a medium score, Kayin is able to secure the loan with a rather high interest rate.

Below are the rates at which Ada, Mariam, and Kayin, are able to borrow money.

Loan Applicant	Loan Amount	Credit Score Out of 999	Interest Rate	Interest Repaid	Total Loan & Interest Paid
Ada	15,000	940	5.8%	2,316	17,316
Mariam	15,000	780	8.9%	3,639	18,639
Kayin	15,000	630	22.3%	10,011	25,011

Fatima, the spender, unfortunately, faces significant challenges due to her poor credit history. With a track record of late payments and defaults, her loan application is flat-out rejected, and her credit score sits at a low 450.

The experiences of these individuals highlight the importance of an excellent credit history. Ada and Kayin borrowed the same amount over the same period, but Kayin had to pay £7,695 more due to her lower credit score. Poor credit can be costly and impede your path to financial freedom.

In conclusion, credit may seem daunting, but it's a crucial part of our financial lives. Despite some finance books painting all borrowing in a negative light, credit can actually be a tool for financial freedom when used wisely. Whether it's securing a mortgage for your dream home or proving your reliability to landlords, understanding and managing credit is essential.

By knowing how credit works, maintaining good financial habits, and staying informed about your credit file and score, you can navigate the world of credit more confidently. Remember, mistakes happen, but with patience and determination, you can rebuild your credit and improve your financial future. So, embrace credit as a tool for building the life you want, and use it wisely to achieve your goals.

CHAPTER TEN—CORE LESSONS

- Maintaining a good credit history is essential for borrowing. You need to borrow for large purchases like buying a home.
- Timely payments and responsible credit card use positively impact credit scores.
- Not having any credit history is a disadvantage. Lenders have no track record to assess your creditworthiness.
- Joint credit applications with someone with bad credit can affect your credit negatively.
- Checking and monitoring your credit report is essential for accuracy.
- Bad credit can lead to higher costs and delays in financial freedom.
- Registering on the electoral roll can positively impact your credit rating.

Chapter Ten—Exercise

Think about one action you can take today to improve your credit history. It could be setting up automatic bill payments, paying down one outstanding debt, or checking your credit report for errors. Write down your chosen action and commit to completing it within the next week. Taking small steps like these can make a significant difference in building a solid credit history.

MAKE A DIFFERENCE WITH YOUR REVIEW

"If you think you are too small to make a difference, you haven't spent the night with a mosquito."
— An African Proverb.

Taking control of your finances and building wealth is empowering. If *The Black Woman's Guide to Building Wealth* has helped you feel this positive shift, you know how transformative it can be.

Remember when managing money felt tough and uncertain? Right now, another Black woman is starting that same journey, looking for the guidance you've found. Your honest review could be the light she needs to take control of her finances.

Why Does Your Review Matter?

- **Representation and Relatability:** This book is written by a Black woman who, like you, has faced financial challenges and grown stronger. Your review helps others see themselves in these pages.
- **Guiding Others:** Many Black women are looking for ways to build wealth. Your review could be the encouragement they need to start their journey.
- **Enhancing Visibility:** Reviews help this book reach more sisters who need it. Your words can make it easier for others to find this resource.

It only takes a minute, but your review could inspire and uplift someone else. Think of it as helping a sister or your younger self.

Ready to make a difference?

Scan the QR code below to leave your review.

Thank you for being part of this journey. Together, we can build a future full of abundance and prosperity for ourselves and our community.

With gratitude,
Joyce

Chapter Eleven

BUYING YOUR HOME AND BUILDING PROPERTY WEALTH

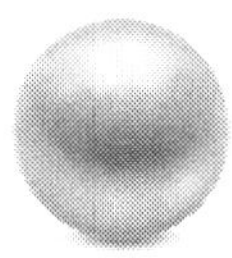

Housing, mortgages, and credit are intertwined; you can't discuss one without delving into the others. In the last chapter, we discussed credit, covering all the ins and outs. Let's now shift our focus to mortgages—the enormous loans that can help you secure your dream home.

Regarding financial milestones, securing your first mortgage is a heavyweight champion demanding your complete attention. Just a little nugget about me: I've got firsthand experience as a former mortgage specialist with the UK's largest lender. So, consider me your ally in this financial journey.

Mortgages don't just get you homes; they're the key to building property wealth. Remember when we talked about net worth? The Black community, on average, has seven times less net worth than others. Property wealth is a big player here. One of the reasons UK Black families have such low net wealth is that only 20% of us own our homes, with the remaining 80% renting and producing wealth for others. This chapter explains why this happens and how we can turn things in our favour.

RENTING VERSUS BUYING YOUR HOME

I've noticed a recent trend: many finance guides are now suggesting that renting is better than buying a home. I get where they're coming from—mortgages are big loans, and if not handled properly, they can mess up your finances. Plus, saving for a huge deposit is no small feat. So, these well-meaning gurus say, "It's too hard to save nowadays. Just rent for the rest of your life.

But hold on a minute. Let's think about who's giving this advice. Many of these finance experts are most likely homeowners, probably with multiple properties, and would love nothing more than to be your landlord forever.

Don't buy into this mindset. Yes, saving for a deposit is tough, and home prices are skyrocketing. But if you manage your mortgage well, your home becomes an asset you own by the end of the term. So, instead of settling for a lifetime of renting, let's up our saving game and aim for ownership. It's challenging, but owning your home can be a powerful step towards building your wealth.

We all need a place to live, whether it is rented or owned. Housing costs are just part of being a responsible, working adult. Unless you fancy still living with your parents at 40 and dealing with all the drawbacks of being bossed around by mum. So, if you know you've got to pay for housing, why not aim to own it as soon as possible?

The whole "rent instead of own" advice doesn't quite add up when you realise that, according to Halifax, one of the UK's major mortgage lenders, owning works out cheaper than renting in the long run (Halifax, 2023). Let that sink in.

The table below shows the difference between owning and renting from 2012 to 2022:

Year	Average Monthly Homeowning Cost	Average Monthly Rent Payment	Annual Savings for Owners
2012	£614	£661	£572
2013	£581	£692	£1,327
2014	£607	£720	£1,361
2015	£616	£744	£1,539
2016	£629	£759	£1,567
2017	£629	£754	£1,501
2018	£669	£759	£1,084
2019	£727	£747	£238
2020	£744	£821	£923
2021	£766	£874	£1,300
2022	£971	£1,013	£498

The main disadvantage of renting is that you pay more and have no assets to show for all your payments.

Renting may work for certain people, but within the Black community, let's do everything possible to buy our homes.

Summing up the perks of owning your home:

1. **Equity Building:** With every mortgage payment you make, you own more of your home. By the end of the mortgage term, the property is a valuable asset in your name. Renting gives you nothing back but builds wealth for your landlord.
2. **Stability:** Unlike renting, owning a home provides a sense of stability. You're not at the mercy of your landlord's decisions and have control over your living space.
3. **Personalisation:** It's your space! Paint the walls, plant a garden, or knock down a wall (within reason, of course). Homeownership allows you to customise your living space to fit your style and needs.

4. **Potential Investment:** Property values in the UK tend to rise over time due to limited land and high demand. While markets may fluctuate in the short term, the long-term trend is typically upward. Focus on the bigger picture—property ownership is a long-term investment that grows in value and pays off over time.
5. **Predictable Payments:** Unlike renting, where the landlord can increase your rent, a fixed-rate mortgage ensures consistent monthly payments, making budgeting more predictable.
6. **Community Connection:** Owning a home means putting down roots in a community. This can lead to a stronger sense of belonging and connection.
7. **Freedom to Rent:** If you have extra space, you can rent it out for additional income, helping with mortgage payments or other expenses.
8. **Retirement Nest Egg:** Owning a home can be crucial to your retirement plan. Housing costs decrease once the mortgage is paid off, providing financial relief during retirement.
9. **Sense of Achievement:** Finally, there's the pride and satisfaction of homeownership. It's a significant life milestone and a tangible representation of your hard work and financial responsibility.
10. **Generational Wealth:** Owning a home builds generational wealth by passing down properties to heirs.

CHALLENGES TO HOMEOWNERSHIP

Obtaining a mortgage comes with significant challenges. However, much like anything worthwhile in life, challenges are inevitable. Our ability to face and conquer these challenges propels us toward reaching our full potential. This is a fundamental principle of growth.

1. **Skyrocketing Property Prices:** Buying a home, particularly in prominent cities like London, comes with an exorbitant price tag,

posing a significant hurdle for numerous Black families aiming to climb the property ladder. The challenge intensifies within our community as a majority of Black families opt for city living over more affordable regions in the UK.

2. **Deposit Requirements:** Saving for a substantial deposit is a significant hurdle for potential homebuyers, particularly first-time buyers. In South East England, the average deposit is £97,320 (Halifax, 2023). Saving £1,000 presents a challenge for many, let alone the daunting task of saving £100,000. Most give up before even trying.
3. **Income Challenges:** Qualifying for a mortgage is tough, especially when it comes to income. For Black women, it's even harder as we're less likely to be top earners (London School of Economics and Political Science, 2021), and many of us are sole parents (Office for National Statistics, 2023). As a single parent, my job stability was impacted—I had to turn down certain roles to balance work and family, and taking time off for my kids affected my chances for promotion. Mummy duties always came first.
4. **Navigating Credit Ratings:** Many people grasp the significance of a robust credit history, but there's often some confusion about what factors improve our credit. Basic actions like exceeding 30% of our credit limit or not settling our credit card bill in full when due can dent our credit history. Plus, quite a few people are in the dark about how long credit scores take to bounce back.
5. **Limited or No Access to the Bank of Mum and Dad:** The Bank of Mum and Dad is a term used to describe a situation where parents or family members provide financial assistance, typically in the form of a loan or gift, to their adult children to help them with significant life expenses like buying a home. Sadly, there are not a lot of Black families that can afford the gift of money to their children. In fact, the situation is often reversed, with younger family members taking on responsibilities to support their relatives in various forms of Black tax.

GETTING ON THE PROPERTY LADDER

Right, we've discussed the common challenges to homeownership and obtaining a mortgage to make our dreams come true. Let's shift our attention to how to get on the property ladder. As hard as homeownership feels, others manage to get on the property ladder just fine. With a little organisation and strategic planning, we, too, can own our dream homes.

Organise Your Finances

There's no magical solution here; success hinges on putting in the effort and establishing solid fundamentals.

Increase your Income: First on the agenda is to boost your income. I understand it's easier said than done; however, don't throw in the towel. Actively seek out opportunities for promotion.

The following story marks another major milestone in my financial breakthrough, and I hope it inspires you.

As I was trying to get my finances in order, I cut back on spending as much as I could until I couldn't cut anymore. Any more cuts would have me walking around barefoot!

I had to find a way to bring in more money. Instead of hunting for a new job, I decided to work with what I had. A bird in hand and all that. My then-boss was a really smart woman, so I couldn't just ask for a raise out of the blue. I had to prove I deserved it by helping the company save money or make more.

I came up with a plan to save money and showed this plan to my boss. I suggested that if I could make these savings happen, then I'd deserve a raise. My boss agreed.

I exceeded targets, securing deals that cut costs by 80%. This achievement earned me a 33% raise and a promotion, providing a significant boost to my financial journey.

I share this story to inspire you to find ways to earn more money, even if you're unsure where to start. I had my doubts too, but I decided to give it a try. The path to making extra cash varies for everyone. What matters most is believing that you can. Think of your mind as a problem-solving machine. Ask yourself, "How can I make more money?" Soon, you'll be brainstorming all the ways to boost your income.

Save for Deposit and Fees: Saving can feel like a challenge, especially with a hefty goal of £100,000, but it's not just about the amount—building the habit is vital. The more you save for your deposit, the better mortgage deals open up. While the minimum deposit is 5%, aim higher; shoot for 10%.

Don't forget about mortgage fees; I'll cover those later in this chapter. We'll explore schemes like the Springboard Mortgage, a great way to get a boost from friends and family for your deposit. Make the most of government schemes to make saving smoother. Look into incentives like LISA (we'll discuss this later) and schemes rewarding your saving efforts.

Most importantly, start early. Use every resource available, whether it's support from parents or government schemes.

Control Your Spending: Your ability to save will affect your spending. Spending and saving sit in opposite corners of a boxing ring. One of these needs to come out victorious. Which would it be for you?

Manage Your Debts: Taking control of all other debts is paramount. Lenders consider your entire financial picture when offering a mortgage. The more outstanding loans and credit card balances you have, the less they'll be willing to lend. A mortgage is a heavyweight in the financial realm—treat it like a significant houseguest. Getting your finances in order is crucial before diving into a mortgage. Aim for no money left owing on your credit cards—that's an ideal goal. It's okay to use credit cards; just make sure to pay off what you spend every month.

Check Your Credit Score: Borrowing a lot of money relies on having a good credit history. It's never too early to start thinking about this—I'd say as soon as you turn 18. Young people usually don't have much credit history until they're old enough for a bank account and credit card.

Be smart about building credit. Avoid common mistakes like maxing out credit cards or paying bills late. At 18, get on the electoral roll—it helps build your credit.

Before you plan to buy a home, check your credit report. You don't want to be excited and then find out your credit isn't great. Fixing bad credit can take a long time. If your credit is already good, keep it that way. The better your credit, the better deals you get from lenders—lower interest rates and maybe even more money.

If your credit isn't great, don't worry. Follow the tips in this book to help fix it and start immediately. I suggest keeping an eye on your credit score three years before you plan to buy. That way, you have time to improve your credit.

FIND AFFORDABLE HOMES OUTSIDE THE CITY

Statistics show a striking tendency. Most Black households prefer to live in London over other parts of the UK. London housing prices are far higher than in other parts of the UK and continue to rise. The ever-increasing house costs in London make homeownership nearly impossible unless you are pretty wealthy.

The table provided shows the variation in average prices for a three-bedroom house across various UK regions, as reported by Halifax in 2023.

UK Regions	Average House Price	Average Mortgage	Average Deposit
Greater London	587,733	399,070	188,663
South East	393,259	295,938	97,321
East of England	355,770	268,613	87,157
South West	298,937	223,899	75,038
East Midlands	237,262	185,571	51,691
West Midlands	236,837	184,568	52,269
North West	215,236	171,463	43,773
Yorkshire & Humberside	201,283	160,090	41,193
Wales	198,710	163,187	35,523
Scotland	195,449	162,161	33,288
North East	172,780	139,860	32,920
Northern Ireland	164,660	131,526	33,134

A three-bedroom house in London could buy you three houses in other parts of the UK.

Why Homeownership is a Challenge Within Our Community

- **Location Preference:** We prefer living in major cities like London, where the average cost of homes is around £600,000.
- **Income Bracket**: 79% of Black households fall into the lowest income bracket.
- **The Challenge:** Low income + high living costs = tough homeownership.
- **Current Homeownership Rate:** Only 20% of Black households own homes.
- **Solution:** Consider affordable housing options outside London to boost homeownership rates.

Contrast with the UK Asian Community:

- **Homeownership Rate:** 45%
- **Strategy:** Spread across the UK, not just in costly cities like London, allowing them to buy homes at lower costs (Office for National Statistics, 2020).

GOVERNMENT HELP TO FIND YOUR HOME

The UK government has a range of initiatives to support your journey to homeownership. Some provide discounts to ease the financial burden of buying a home, while others help you save for your property, offering perks like guaranteed interest or bonuses to grow your savings.

Some schemes have expired, such as the Help to Buy equity loan in England. The good news is that if you have already signed up, you are still eligible for the advantages. Also, watch for the launch of new schemes. Check online regularly for the most recent home-buying programs.

Right to Buy

Currently, 44% of Black families live in social housing (Gov.UK, 2021). This situation presents a unique advantage through government initiatives like the Right to Buy (RTB) scheme. Depending on your tenancy type, you might have the opportunity to buy your council apartment with a massive discount on the property's value. Having a Right to Buy your council home isn't something to dismiss lightly. I've seen many start their home ownership journeys with their council homes. Some are happy to live in the flats for the rest of their lives, while others trade up to larger homes.

The Right to Buy (RTB) scheme often comes with a substantial discount; the discount you get depends on your borough and how long you've lived there. Discounts can reach hundreds of thousands. Get the most up-to-date information at the GOV.UK website.

If you're a council tenant but your current apartment isn't eligible for the Right to Buy scheme—for instance, if you reside in a Housing Association apartment, where the RTB option is typically unavailable—consider exploring exchanges with other council residents who have the right to buy. Websites like HomeSwapper.co.uk and Council-exchange.co.uk can guide you through this process.

Shared Ownership

If saving up for a full deposit and making high mortgage payments for your ideal home seem out of reach, shared ownership could be the solution. In the United Kingdom, this plan allows you to buy a portion of a property while renting the remainder. From September 2020, the minimum initial share you can buy in a property was reduced from 25% to 10%. Furthermore, you can buy additional shares in 1% instalments with significantly lower fees.

1. **Lower Entry Costs:** Shared ownership provides a pathway to the property market with a lower deposit. Getting a mortgage for the portion you're buying is more straightforward. For example, buying 20% of a £400,000 flat works out at £80,000. Obtaining a mortgage for a £80,000 property is more manageable than one for £400,000. Your required deposit for this share is lower at £8,000 compared to £40,000. This not only eases the financial burden but also makes the dream of homeownership a reality.
2. **Affordable Monthly Payments:** Your mortgage payments in shared ownership are typically more affordable than outright purchases, leading to manageable monthly costs.

3. **Gradual Ownership:** You can start ownership as low as 10%, with the option to increase it over time, allowing you to steadily progress toward full ownership at your pace. In practical terms, a 10% stake in a £400,000 flat translates to a purchase price of £40,000 for your specific portion.
4. **Shared Maintenance Costs:** Some maintenance expenses are shared with the housing association, alleviating your financial responsibilities.

Get the most up-to-date information at the GOV.UK website.

The Mortgage Guarantee Scheme

The Mortgage Guarantee Scheme is a government-backed program to help people with small deposits buy homes. It's different from a guarantor mortgage, which involves another person vouching for your loan.

Here's how it works:

Imagine you want to buy a house, but your deposit is relatively small. Normally, lenders might be hesitant to approve your loan. Under this scheme, the government steps in and guarantees a part of your loan—specifically, 15% of the amount you borrow. This guarantee is for the lender and not you, ensuring the lender is protected if you fail to make your mortgage payments and the home has to be repossessed.

What does this mean for you? While you still borrow the full amount needed to buy your home, the government guarantee makes lenders more willing to offer you a mortgage. It's a win-win for the lender.

The scheme, a valuable opportunity, is available to first-time buyers and existing homeowners who can only afford a deposit between 5% and 9%. The property must be valued at £600,000 or less, and you must be 18 or older. This opportunity lasts only until June 30, 2025. Find out more at gov.uk/the-mortgage-guarantee-scheme.

First Home Scheme

First Home Scheme is a fantastic program for buying your first home. The scheme allows you to buy your first home (assuming you qualify) at a substantial discount, often ranging from 30% to 50% below the market value. This scheme focuses on newly built homes.

To qualify, you need to be at least 18, be a first-time buyer, and be able to get a mortgage for at least half of the home's value. So, if a home's value is £200,000, you must be able to get a mortgage of £100,000 on your own without any assistance.

The scheme aims to help individuals whose total household income does not exceed £80,000 or £90,000 in London.

Local authorities can prioritise specific groups, such as essential workers like nurses, military personnel, and lower-income individuals. Get the most up-to-date information at the GOV.UK website.

A Lifetime ISA (LISA)

A LISA isn't a home discount scheme; it's a savings account designed to help young people save for their first home. It rewards your saving efforts. You can save up to £4,000 each year until you turn 50. The government adds a sweet 25% bonus to your savings, up to a maximum of £1,000 per year. The property you're eyeing must be valued at £450,000 or less. To take advantage of a Lifetime ISA (LISA), you must be between 18 and 39 years old. Make sure to make your first payment into your LISA before you turn 40. If you and another first-time buyer have LISAs, you can combine them to buy the same property. Get the most up-to-date information at the GOV.UK website.

HOW MUCH CAN YOU BORROW?

When applying for a mortgage on your own, lenders typically determine the loan amount based on a multiple of your annual income. The better your credit score, the higher the multiple. A poor credit score will limit the amount a lender is willing to offer. The precise loan amount extended by lenders will depend upon their internal procedures.

Lenders also evaluate existing debts. The more debts you carry, the less money a lender will lend. This consideration is rooted in your ability to manage financial commitments; excessive debts will raise concerns about your capacity to meet monthly mortgage payments.

Sole Mortgage Application

Lenders can lend up to 4.5 times an individual's annual salary. For example, with an annual salary of £40,000, the potential loan amount could be £180,000 (£40,000 x 4.5). This figure is an estimate, subject to the lender's specific criteria.

Joint Ownership Application

When two people apply for a mortgage together, the bank decides how much money to lend based on joint earnings. Lending criteria vary from bank to bank, but they usually use a multiple between 3.5 and 4 times the total earnings of both people. So, if both people make £70,000 a year together, they might be able to borrow between £245,000 and £280,000.

Getting a mortgage together has advantages. You can borrow more money, making getting the home you want easier. The bank likes it when two people pay back one mortgage. It makes the mortgage more secure for the bank. They also check both people's credit histories.

But be careful! Before you decide to get a mortgage together, make sure you know about the other person's credit history and let them know about yours. Joint mortgages are typically taken out by couples.

Joint-Borrower-Sole-Proprietor Mortgage

A joint-borrower-sole-proprietor (JBSP) mortgage allows a person with a low income to use other people's income to get a bigger mortgage. Joint borrowers could include parents, siblings, or friends buying a home together. You can have up to four people on this mortgage. Everyone's income is combined to get a larger loan. A JBSP makes buying a home easier.

Even though multiple people are on the mortgage, only one person owns the home. However, keep in mind that everyone in a JBSP mortgage is equally responsible for paying back the mortgage. From the lender's point of view, having multiple borrowers is good news. They have more people to go after if the legal owner cannot make payments.

Consider a young woman who dreams of owning a £300,000 flat, but her £ 30,000 salary limits her mortgage to £ 165,000. She can secure a larger loan with her mother's support in a JBSP mortgage. Their combined income of £ 100,000 allows them to borrow up to £400,000, making the flat within reach.

Here are the advantages for this young borrower just starting out:

- She can afford a more expensive flat with help from a relative.
- If the parent has a good credit rating, it boosts the daughter's credit rating.

- The daughter is the home's legal owner, even though the parent helped secure a larger mortgage.
- Any increase in property value belongs to the daughter.
- The parent is responsible for mortgage payments if the daughter can't make them.
- The daughter can take over the whole mortgage later when her income increases.
- With help from her mum, the daughter can get on the property ladder sooner, avoiding rising property prices.

I'd be the first to admit that JBSP is an act of love. The mum is a joint borrower but does not get any financial benefit; it is sacrificial on the mum's part because all the benefits go to the daughter. It's a bit like the "Bank of Mum and Dad." The JBSP is a unique way for parents to help their kids.

While the idea of a JBSP mortgage is appealing, be mindful of the potential risks. The joint borrowers cover the mortgage payment if the legal owner defaults on payments. So, it's crucial to weigh up the options and proceed cautiously, especially if the borrower has shown financial irresponsibility in the past. Nothing damages relationships like money.

Despite the risks, I love this idea; it's new and wasn't around when I was a mortgage adviser. It's a win for young people getting on the property ladder with some help from their parents.

Guarantor Mortgages

Guarantor mortgages work like joint-borrower-sole-proprietor mortgages and have been around for a while. Essentially, your guarantor, usually a parent, must cover your mortgage payments if you can't manage them. Your guarantor is not the legal owner of your property.

Unlike joint-borrower-sole-proprietor mortgages, the application is not based on joint salaries. Your guarantor puts their mortgage-free home or savings on the line as security for your mortgage. They commit to covering the payments if you can't pay. They can lose their home or savings if you don't pay your mortgage.

Your guarantor needs to have a solid credit history. This ensures lenders trust their financial reliability. Some banks will insist the guarantor talks to a legal expert to be sure they understand the risks.

Guarantor mortgages can be helpful in a few situations:

- If you don't earn much.
- If you lack a substantial deposit, having a guarantor could potentially enable you to secure the entire home loan.
- If your credit score isn't great, having a guarantor makes lenders more likely to lend to you.
- If you don't have any credit history, your guarantor can vouch for you.

If you're thinking about a guarantor mortgage, be sure to think it through. Your guarantor could lose their savings or even their home if you can't make your mortgage payments. Everyone involved needs to be super clear about what's expected. If you ever struggle to pay on a guarantor mortgage, speaking up as soon as possible is important because your guarantor's assets are at risk.

Springboard Mortgages

A springboard mortgage is when your family or friends help you with the money needed for a home deposit. Here's how it works:

1. **Deposit Help:** Instead of you coming up with the hefty deposit, your family or friends put a chunk of their money into a special

savings account connected to your mortgage. This money acts like a safety net or collateral.

2. **Less Deposit:** With this setup, you can get a mortgage with a smaller or sometimes no deposit.
3. **Interest Earning:** Depending on the deal, the money in the linked account might earn interest.
4. **Money returned:** The owner of the money will get the money back after a while, usually when you've built up enough ownership in the home, which means you've made payments to the mortgage and reduced the original loan substantially.

Springboard Mortgages are handy for people who for some reason cannot save a deposit. It's not the same as a guarantor mortgage because the family or friend who gave the money doesn't have to pay your mortgage if things go wrong. They're only responsible for the money in the linked savings account. To sum it up, both types involve help from family or friends, but in a springboard mortgage, they give a lump sum for the deposit without taking on the legal responsibility for the mortgage. In a guarantor mortgage, the helper takes on more risk by agreeing to pay the mortgage if you can't.

WHAT FEES WILL YOU HAVE TO PAY FOR YOUR MORTGAGE

Getting a mortgage is costly, and it often ends up being more than we think. Some fees might pop up unexpectedly, so it's wise to set aside some extra money just in case. If no surprise fees come up, that's a bonus! Now, here are the usual fees to watch out for:

Mortgage Arrangement/Booking Fee between £1,000 and £2,000	This is a fee the lender charges to set up the loan. It could be a flat fee or a percentage of your loan. Some lenders let you add this fee to the mortgage.
Valuation Fee between £150 and £500	A fee to check that the home you're buying is worth what you're paying.

Survey Fees, also known as Homebuyer Survey, between £500 and £1,500	A fee for checking the home to find any hidden problems before you buy it.
Mortgage Broker Fee between £250 and £2,000	Brokers can charge a fee or receive a commission from the lender. The fee could be a flat fee or a percentage of the loan amount. You don't pay a broker fee if you go directly to a bank for your mortgage.
Legal or conveyancing Fees between £500 and £2,000	A solicitor will handle the legal work of buying a property. Fees depend on the complexity of the transaction and the solicitor's rates.
Land Registry Fees	The Land Registry fee is a charge for registering the property in your name after you buy it.
Mortgage Indemnity Guarantee fee varies. Check with your lender.	Mortgage Indemnity Insurance is a type of insurance that protects the lender if the borrower can't repay the mortgage. It's often required when the deposit is small.
Electronic Transfer Fee between £30 and £50	Electronic fees are charges for moving money from your lender to the seller's solicitor when buying your home. This transfer usually happens on the same day.

Stamp duty is a tax you pay when you buy a property in England or Northern Ireland. First-time buyers get better rates than those buying subsequent homes.

First-time buyer's stamp duty:

Stamp duty on homes up to £425,000	0%
Stamp duty on homes between £425,000–£625,000	5%
Stamp duty on homes over £625,000	Standard rate

Home movers pay different stamp duty rates when buying a second home or any property that isn't their first.

Stamp duty on homes from £0–£250,000	0%
Stamp duty on homes from £250,001–£925,000	5%
Stamp duty on homes from £925,001–£1.5m	10%
Home purchases more than £1.5m	12%

Get the most up-to-date information at the GOV.UK website.

Important Mortgage Terms

- **Interest Rate:** The fee you pay the bank for borrowing money.
- **Fixed Interest Rate:** You can choose a fixed interest rate, where your payments stay the same for a set period, such as two, five, or ten years, making it easier to budget. However, you're locked into the deal for that term. Most lenders let you overpay up to 10% of your mortgage yearly, either in lump sums or monthly, but you can't fully pay off your mortgage during the fixed term.
- **Variable Interest Rate:** A variable interest rate means your payment can increase or decrease. Who might like this? Some prefer it because it's often lower than a fixed rate, helping them reduce their payments. Others like the flexibility, especially if they expect rates to drop or plan to sell or refinance soon. However, with a variable rate, you must be comfortable with the risk of rising rates and able to afford higher payments.

Within the variable rate family, there are different types:

1. **Standard Variable Rate**
   - What it is: The default interest rate set by the lender, it can change at any time, is typically influenced by overall fluctuations in the interest rate market.
   - How it works: Your mortgage rate fluctuates based on market fluctuations, and your monthly payments change accordingly.
2. **Tracker Rate**
   - What it is: This rate "tracks" or follows a specific interest rate, like the Bank of England's base rate. If the benchmark rate goes up, so does your mortgage rate, and vice versa.
   - How it works: Your interest rate moves with changes in the chosen benchmark.

3. **Discounted Variable Rate**
   - What it is: This is a variable rate with a discount from the lender's standard variable rate for a certain period.
   - How it works: Your interest rate is lower than the standard variable rate for a set time, giving you a discount. After the discounted period, it usually reverts to the standard variable rate.
4. **Capped Rate**
   - What it is: This is a variable-rate mortgage, but there's a cap or maximum limit on how high the interest rate can go during a specified period.
   - How it works: Your interest rate can fluctuate within a range, but it won't go above the capped limit.

Regardless of your interest rate type, aim for the lowest possible rate. When your current rate expires, check for new offers. Don't simply accept the rate your current lender offers. Check the rates offered by other lenders. Switching lenders after an offer expires often saves you money.

Interest Only Mortgage

What It Is: You only pay off the interest on the loan, not the loan itself (the capital). For example, if you borrow £100,000 and only pay the interest for 25 years, you still owe a total of £100,000. The borrowed amount doesn't decrease during those 25 years.

Who Might Choose an Interest-Only Mortgage? The most common reason is to have lower monthly payments. Lenders are careful with these mortgages because there's a risk of being unable to pay off the loan at the end of its term. Lenders usually insist on seeing a solid plan for repaying the principal when the term ends.

I've seen interest-only mortgages work well for borrowers who use their yearly bonuses, savings, investments, or pensions to pay down the principal.

Repayment Mortgage

With a repayment mortgage, you pay back both the capital and interest. Each month, your payment reduces both the loan amount and interest, gradually repaying the entire loan.

Who Might Choose a Repayment Mortgage? Lenders prefer this type of mortgage because, while monthly payments may be higher, the mortgage is guaranteed to be paid off at the end of the term. You own more of your home with each payment. By the end of the term, you fully own your property, building valuable equity.

MORTGAGE BEST PRACTICES

At the beginning of this chapter, I talked about how some finance experts suggest renting instead of buying. I don't quite agree with that perspective, but I understand their advice comes from a good place. Buying our homes can be a real financial shock to the system. Considering the significant financial commitment it involves, it's wise to explore the best ways to side-step common pitfalls and get the most out of this hefty financial decision.

Borrowing Too Much Money

I've shared ways to secure bigger loans for your dream home. One such way is the joint-borrower-sole-proprietor mortgage scheme (JBSP). Let's revisit the example of a mum assisting her daughter using JBSP to buy her flat. With their combined salary of £100,000, they secured a £270,000 mortgage for her dream home.

The table below highlights a problem. The monthly mortgage payment consumes approximately 75% of the daughter's net monthly income. This payment does not include other essentials like council tax, utilities, insurance, food or travel. Cast your mind back to the budget chapter. The 50/30/20 recommends that all essentials should not exceed 50 of net income. Okay, so, lets' say the 50/30/20 is a bit extreme in today's economy. Another strategy is the 70/10/10. Still way too high for just the mortgage payment.

Scenario	Details
Monthly Mortgage Payment @ 4.99% over 25 years	£1,577
Monthly Net Salary	£2,093
Percentage of Net Salary	75% of net salary
Additional Costs Not Included	Home insurance, council tax, and other essential living expenses.
Risk	The young lady cannot afford to pay this mortgage and is likely to default.

Share the Burden

A good solution will be to share the burden of the mortgage. Many mortgage lenders allow you to have a lodger as long as you live in the property. But don't just assume; check that having a lodger aligns with your mortgage T&Cs. The good news is that having a lodger won't affect your mortgage interest rate or monthly payments. In our example, it would be wise for the borrower to purchase a two-bedroom flat to rent the spare room, which can help share the costs.

Extend Your Mortgage Term to Reduce Monthly Payments

Extending the mortgage term offers much-needed flexibility, especially at the beginning when budgets are often tight. While a longer term in this scenario means paying more interest—up to £151,000 more—the lower monthly payments provide breathing room when it's most needed. The good news is that there are ways to reduce the overall cost and shorten the term over time, helping you save money in the long run.

Current Mortgage Term	25 years
Current Monthly Payment	£1,577
Total Interest Payable (25-Year Term)	£203,046
Proposed Solution	Extend mortgage term to 40 years
New Monthly Payment	£1,300
Total Interest Payable (40-Year Term)	£354,069
Difference in Interest (25 vs 40 Years)	£151,000 increase
Trade-Off	Lower monthly payments now, but significantly higher interest costs over time

Pay Extra into Your Mortgage

Most lenders allow borrowers to overpay up to 10% of their mortgage annually. While the young lady in our scenario may not have extra funds at the start of her mortgage, it's reasonable to expect her income to grow over time. As it does, she can use some of the surplus to make extra payments on her mortgage beyond the regular monthly payments. The table below illustrates the significant impact of paying just £100 or £200 extra each month on a £270,000 mortgage with a 40-year term.

Overpayment Amount	Interest Savings	Term Reduction
No Overpayment	£0	No Reduction
£100 Extra Per Month	£77,000	7 years, 5 months
£200 Extra Per Month	£125,000	12 years, 2 months

The key takeaway is simple: the more you overpay, the more you save on interest, and the quicker you clear your mortgage. If you can overpay the maximum allowed (usually 10% per year), you could be mortgage-free in less than 10 years. Just ensure your mortgage permits overpayments and that every extra payment goes directly towards the principal. This strategy could save you a significant amount in interest over the life of your mortgage.

Be mindful of lifestyle creep—the tendency to spend more as your income grows. This can be a significant factor in managing your mortgage effectively. As discussed in the budget chapter, discretionary spending can distract you from your financial goals. A smart goal is to eliminate all debt as quickly as possible, and that includes your mortgage. Even though it's a necessary debt, it's still a debt. Set the intention early on that as your income rises, you'll funnel those extra funds into paying off your mortgage faster.

Start Early

Lenders prefer borrowers with stable jobs and typically avoid mortgages that extend beyond retirement, usually around age 65. If you're under 25, you might qualify for a 40-year term. But if you're over 40, lenders may shorten the term to match your retirement age.

A shorter term means higher monthly payments, which could reduce the loan amount lenders are willing to offer to keep payments affordable.

Save Up for Emergencies

At the beginning of your mortgage journey, your savings would have taken a hit—mortgages can be quite the financial undertaking. However, there's no time for complacency. The game has changed; you're a responsible adult with a mortgage. This means you are in charge of fixing things. No more calling on Mum or Dad to fix things, and certainly, no landlord to sort out that broken boiler. You're now the boss, handling everything from a leaky tap to broken windows.

Get ready for these expenses. Rebuild your emergency funds to tackle the unforeseen costs that will show up. Trust me, they will show up. Neglecting to replenish your rainy-day funds will lead to debt when emergencies inevitably crop up.

Stay Away from Additional Debts

It's natural to want to deck out our new place, especially when the excitement of ownership sets in. It's an emotional time, a significant achievement, and it's easy to get carried away with borrowing more to create the perfect look. However, resist the urge. Enjoy the peace of having only your mortgage as your primary financial commitment for a while.

Resist the thought that your old furniture is not good enough and that every appliance must be brand spanking new. Banks will fall over themselves to offer you extra loans. RESIST! Trust me, owning a home is a massive accomplishment in today's economic climate; you don't need to impress anyone with new matching furniture. Consider buying second-hand if you've never owned furniture before. Friends and family are already impressed with your home purchase; there is no need to borrow more for fancy furnishings.

Remember, as far as commitment goes, your mortgage is a heavyweight. Recover from the shocking expense of a new home before splurging on shiny new gizmos.

Real-Life Application: Janet and Talia

Janet and Talia

Talia and Janet, best friends and work buddies for two decades, practically do everything together. They share holidays, hang out beyond the office, and weather life's ups and downs. They even coincidentally bought homes around the same time.

Despite their tight bond, their money strategies differ. One might think Talia's rolling in it at a glance—her wardrobe and home are like something out of a glossy magazine. Janet, on the other hand, is more down-to-earth. She's not flashy, but she's not shabby either. She's the master of finding that sweet spot between splurging and saving.

Janet's financial strategy revolves around savings and debt clearance. With a modest income, she knows job security is a thing of the past, so she diligently channels extra cash into her mortgage and savings. Following her mum's wise words, "The borrower is a slave to the lender," Janet wants no part of that slavery.

In contrast, Talia enjoys the finer things—looking and smelling good—living in what feels like a posh showroom. Her motto? *"Live for today, 'cause who knows what tomorrow brings?"* Saving? Not her thing. *"What's the point? I could die tomorrow."* Extra mortgage payments hold no appeal for her either.

Finance management is a bone of contention between the friends. Janet preaches the value of financial responsibility, but Talia dislikes being preached to. To preserve their friendship, Janet eases off on the money talks.

Then, the unexpected happened in 2020—both ladies were made redundant due to the COVID-19 epidemic. This was a shock for the two friends who thought their jobs were secure, given their many years of service and experience. Ironically, they were the first to be shown the door, with minimal compensation.

With their different financial philosophies, you can bet their reactions to redundancy are poles apart.

Janet's Post-redundancy Plans: Janet had fully paid her mortgage earlier than expected because she was making extra payments. She was prepared for emergencies like this. After the shock wore off, she decided to take a much-needed break before searching for a new job. She thought reconnecting with her Jamaican roots would be a great idea. She hadn't seen her cousins in 20 years. So, off she went, taking the chance to enjoy the laid-back life on the beautiful island.

During her time away, she explored other Caribbean islands, relaxing on sandy beaches and swimming in turquoise waters. She had always wanted to do this but never had the time or money. Now, she could check these off her to-do list.

She rented out her mortgage-free home in the UK to support her island adventure. The rent covered all her expenses and even left some extra monthly money. Surprisingly, losing her job turned out to be a blessing in disguise.

Now, Janet is thinking about her next steps—maybe starting her own business or finding another job. But for now, she's just taking it easy and enjoying life in the Caribbean.

Talia's Post-redundancy Plans: Talia's plans radically differed from those of her best friend, Janet. She faced some tough challenges. Her mortgage was behind, and she had four maxed-out credit cards. She might lose her home if she didn't catch up on her payments. So, getting a job pronto became her top priority.

However, job hunting was new and confusing for Talia since she hadn't done it in the last 20 years. She also worried that her age, gender, and race could make finding a job even harder.

It took Talia six long months, but she did manage to find a job. A job she hated, but had to do to keep on top of her debt payments.

"Now I get what Janet has always told me about debt being an enslaver." Talia feels chained to her desk because her debts control her life. Meanwhile, Janet is living her best life, and Talia wishes she had followed her friend's advice.

Talia now shares the important lesson of managing debt wisely and saving with anyone who will listen. She points to Janet as a great example—owning her home outright and being rich in property.

When we first buy our home, the bank owns most of it. With our regular monthly mortgage payments, we gradually own more of our home each month. By paying more than the regular monthly amount, we start lowering the principal immediately, which builds up your property wealth, aka equity, much faster.

It's a win-win situation: you increase your property wealth, cut down the overall interest you pay, and significantly reduce the loan term.

In a nutshell, this chapter's main idea is to champion owning homes instead of renting. I got the info from a 2021 report by the Office for National Statistics, which shines a light on how the Black community, and especially Black women, lags behind in wealth. The report saw homeownership as a vital measure. Though it's been a bit of a long read, as always, I've condensed the crucial points for us to remember.

CHAPTER ELEVEN—CORE LESSONS

- Owning your home is a crucial component of building wealth. Renting? Well, that's making someone else rich. So, do all you can to hop on the homeownership ladder.
- Think of a mortgage as a necessary evil. Necessary because most of us can't splash out all the cash needed to buy a home upfront;

evil because it's a long-term debt that has the potential to keep us bound to work when we would rather be out living our best lives. Remember Talia?

- Before diving into the mortgage world, sort out your financial game plan. Save up and make sure your credit game is strong—it'll make the mortgage journey smoother.
- Be a savvy shopper when hunting for a home. Explore options for snagging affordable homes. Government perks? Grab 'em. If the Bank of Mum and Dad is in play, why not? Look into mortgage schemes that can give you a boost in getting the money you need.
- Steer clear of unnecessary extra debts. Make paying off that mortgage your top priority.
- Use mortgage overpayment calculators. These little wonders show you how chipping in a bit extra here and there cuts down the interest you pay and shortens the time it takes to own your home. Check out calculators like the one on MoneySupermarket for a handy guide.

Chapter Eleven—Exercise

For those diving into homeownership for the first time:

1. Start by checking your credit file to make sure it's in tip-top shape. If not, head back to the Building Credit chapter for tips on improving it.
2. Explore all available government help and saving schemes, picking the ones that match your goals.
3. Get down to budgeting. Create a plan with a dedicated line for saving toward your home down payment.
4. If you've got other debts, create a strategy to clear those before jumping into a mortgage.

Now, for those who are already proud homeowners:

1. Fire up that mortgage repayment calculator. See how a little extra payment on top of your usual monthly mortgage can shrink your overall interest and shorten the mortgage term.
2. Get down to budgeting—craft a plan that allocates a specific portion for saving, aiming to make extra payments to clear your mortgage earlier than scheduled.
3. Picture what your life will feel like if you no longer have monthly mortgage payments because you've paid them off ahead of schedule! Grab a journal and write what you would do with that financial freedom. Would you take a break, perhaps travel, and visit places you've always wanted to go? Just one monthly mortgage payment is enough for a nice break. Paying your mortgage off means you can take 12 nice breaks a year.

Chapter Twelve

PERSONAL LOANS

Once upon a time, purchasing a car, planning a wedding, or building an emergency fund meant months, even years, of disciplined saving. Every pound was earned with sweat and spent with caution.

Today, personal loans have changed that. No more waiting or saving; you can have instant cash with just a few clicks. Need money for a big purchase? A personal loan offers it up front, but with one key difference—you'll spend years paying it back, with added interest.

The transition from traditional to modern borrowing methods has made it too easy to bypass the saving phase and jump straight to the spending phase. You no longer need to dress up for a meeting with the bank manager and justify your need for money. It's all online, swift, and almost effortless.

However, this convenience comes with a hefty price tag. The instant availability of loans can promote reckless spending and a mounting debt problem. What once demanded discipline and meticulous planning is now just a few clicks away, making it easy to overlook the long-term repercussions.

Making big purchases on a low income always requires discipline. You either have the discipline to meticulously save or to meticulously repay the loan, but a loan comes with the added cost of interest.

WHEN PERSONAL LOANS CAN BE HANDY

Personal loans can be powerful tools, especially for debt consolidation or improving your home. However, having a well-thought-out plan for repaying the loan is super important.

Combining Debts (also known as debt consolidation): If you've got many small debts with high interest rates, such as credit card bills, store cards, and other debts, it's a good idea to roll them into one personal loan with a lower interest rate. This way, you save money on interest, and it's simpler to handle just one debt instead of many.

Home Improvements: Got plans to spruce up your home? A personal loan can be a good choice to pay for home improvements if the improvements make your home more valuable.

I've seen many instances where people take on loans without a clear plan. These loans often come as a response to growing financial troubles. Here are the most common wrong reasons people take out loans:

- **Frivolous Spending**: People sometimes take out personal loans to splurge on non-essential stuff, like fancy gadgets or extravagant holidays. Some folks do it to show off their wealth or to keep up with the spending habits of friends and family.

- **Robbing Peter to Pay Paul**: This is when loans are used to pay other credits like rent, mortgage, or utility bills. Some folks even use loans to tackle their monthly credit card and other debts. The problem with this approach is that rent, mortgage, and credit card bills show up monthly. If you take out a loan to pay them in January, what happens in February? This pattern creates a never-ending loop of debt and financial stress.
- **Using Personal Loans to Compensate for Low or Unstable Income**: If your income isn't regular or dependable, adding more debt through a personal loan is not the way to go. It's really important to have a stable income to make sure you can handle those monthly repayments.
- **Irresistible Loan Offers**: This is when banks tempt customers into taking loans, often without a clear repayment plan or a genuine need. During my time at the bank, we'd offer loans to customers, including those visiting for routine transactions. Sadly, less financially savvy customers sometimes took the bait, borrowing money they hadn't initially thought they needed. Today, online and app-based loan offers are everywhere. If your bank suddenly dangles a personal loan in front of you, the temptation to accept can be hard to resist.

ESSENTIAL CONSIDERATIONS BEFORE TAKING OUT A PERSONAL LOAN

Applying for a Loan: If you must take out a loan, start with your bank since they can access your records and know your financial situation. Don't stop there, use comparison websites and loan calculators to explore all available options. Make sure you fully understand the loan terms, including any prepayment penalties or how multiple applications might affect your credit score.

Interest Rates and Fees: Interest rates vary based on your credit history, loan amount, and repayment term. It's important to understand whether the rate is fixed or variable and to check the APR, which includes the interest rate and any additional fees. This will give you a clearer picture of the total cost of the loan.

Paying Back: The amount borrowed, the interest rate, and the loan term determine your monthly repayment. Budget carefully to ensure your repayments are affordable, and if you have the option to repay the loan early without a penalty, do so. Early repayment would save you money on interest.

Think About the Risk: Before taking out a loan, understand the risks involved. Debt can quickly spiral out of control if not managed carefully. I've seen people take out a personal loan to pay off their credit cards, only to then max out those cards again, making their debt situation worse.

Defaulting on loan payments is perhaps the biggest risk of all. If you fail to make your loan payments, you will damage your credit score, which means you won't get credit easily in the future. There are also potential legal consequences. Before committing to a personal loan, consider alternatives like borrowing from family, using savings, or exploring options with credit unions.

Your Rights: In the UK, the Financial Conduct Authority (FCA) ensures lenders follow strict rules to protect you, the borrower. You have rights, including clear loan terms, the right to early repayment, a cooling-off period, and the ability to lodge complaints. If need be, the Financial Ombudsman Service can help resolve disputes.

CHAPTER TWELVE—CORE LESSONS

Personal loans can be handy when:

- Combining debts (debt consolidation).
- Making home improvements.

Common wrong reasons people take out loans:

- Frivolous spending.
- Robbing Peter to pay Paul.
- Compensating for low or unstable income.
- Yielding to irresistible loan offers.

Key considerations before taking out a personal loan:

- Determine if the loan improves your financial position.
- Evaluate if it reduces interest costs.
- Assess if it boosts an asset.

Tips for applying for a personal loan:

- Start with your bank, but also explore other offers.
- Scrutinise interest rates and fees.
- Understand repayment terms and flexibility.
- Know your rights as a borrower under FCA regulations in the UK.
- Personal loans can be valuable financial tools if used wisely.
- Have a clear plan for loan repayment.

Chapter Thirteen

PAYDAY LOANS

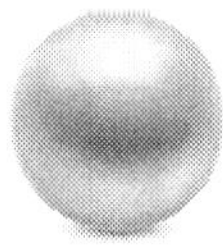

A payday loan is a short-term, small-sum loan that's typically due to be paid back on the borrower's next payday. These loans are designed to provide quick access to cash for people facing unexpected expenses. However, they come with high interest rates and fees, and the total amount to be repaid can be far more than the initial amount borrowed. They are easier to get than a high street bank loan because the lender's rules for lending are more relaxed than those of a bank. Most people who turn to payday lenders often have poor credit or have been turned down by their banks.

Payday loans may promise quick fixes, but the true solution lies in understanding our options and seeking alternatives. Let's step away from the quicksand of predatory lending and build a foundation of financial well-being.

Payday lenders first caught my attention during my daily commute on the London underground. There it was—a poster promising quick money in minutes. But what really struck me was the APR displayed. I thought, *Surely, that must be a typo. There's no way it's right.* But when I checked the company's website, I was stunned to find it was true: 1,596% APR.

It wasn't a mistake. Someone out there was charging people over 1,000% interest on loans. Here I was, complaining about my Barclaycard's interest rate hike to 27%. Unbelievable!

I couldn't help but wonder if it was legal. So, I did some research and discovered that it was perfectly legal as long as the payday company:

- Sticks to a cost cap that limits the interest they can charge.
- Conducts an affordability check.
- Clearly discloses the loan terms.
- Explains the use of continuous payment authority (CPA), a payment collection method.
- Engages in "fair" debt collection practices.

On the FCA website, I found numerous warnings about payday firms operating illegally and being shut down. This told me two things: payday lending is highly lucrative, and, unfortunately, many desperate people expose themselves to these bad players.

WHY DO PEOPLE FALL INTO THIS TRAP?

- **Emergency Financial Needs**: When faced with urgent financial needs, the promise of quick access to cash can be incredibly appealing. The lightning-fast process of obtaining funds becomes a primary motivator.
- **Limited Access to Traditional Credit**: Many individuals turn to payday lenders because they feel they have no choice due to their poor credit history. Payday lenders intentionally make their loans more appealing than banks.
- **Convenience and Ease of Approval**: Borrowers can apply online or in-store with minimal paperwork—an attractive option for those seeking a quick and hassle-free borrowing experience.

- **Lack of Financial Literacy and Awareness**: Lack of awareness about the risks contributes to choosing payday lenders as a seemingly convenient solution. Most people don't know much about interest rates. They just want to know how much they can borrow and what the repayments are.
- **Financial Desperation**: A person in financial trouble might think that payday loans are their only choice. They want the money now and deal with the consequences later.

ARE THERE OTHER OPTIONS?

There are better choices when you're in a difficult money situation.

Below are a few solutions that could help and offer long-term relief so you never have to rely on payday lenders and suffer those wild interest rates:

- **Local Welfare Assistance**: Local authorities in the UK offer welfare assistance programs to provide emergency financial support. Contact your local council to inquire about the availability of grants, loans, or other aid forms.
- **Credit Unions**: Joining a credit union can be a fantastic alternative. Credit unions like My Community Bank, London Mutual Credit Union, or Scotwest Credit Union offer affordable loans, savings accounts, and financial guidance tailored to your needs.
- **Fair for You**: Fair for You is a UK-based social enterprise offering affordable loans for essential household items. They aim to provide a more affordable alternative to high-interest furniture, appliances, and electronics loans.
- **StepChange Debt Charity**: StepChange Debt Charity offers free and confidential advice to individuals struggling with debt. Their expert advisors can help you create a personalised plan to manage your debts and explore alternative solutions.

- **Money Advice Service**: The Money Advice Service is a UK government-funded organisation that offers free and impartial money advice. They provide information, tools, and resources to help you find suitable alternatives to payday loans.
- **Citizens Advice**: Citizens Advice is a network of independent charities across the UK that offers free advice on various issues, including debt management. They can offer debt solutions, and help you negotiate with creditors.

These organisations offer support in times of financial difficulty. Explore your options. You don't have to face it alone—help is available!

OTHER SOURCES OF HELP

Emotional support is just as important in your journey to financial wellness. Here are some ideas to help you maintain a positive mindset.

- **Family and Friends**: Contact trusted, non-judgy family members or friends who can offer a listening ear, advice, and encouragement.
- **Financial Counsellors:** Professional financial counsellors can provide practical advice and emotional support to help you deal with your debt crisis.
- **Therapists or Counsellors**: Mental health professionals can show you ways to cope with the stress and anxiety that often accompany debt.
- **Religious or Spiritual Groups**: If you are part of a trustworthy religious or spiritual community, they can offer support and guidance during tough financial times.
- **Read Finance Books**: Find books like this one that provide insights into personal finance and money management. They are treasures in your hands, offering knowledge and guidance you can return to again and again and follow through on all the exercises.

- **Join Supportive Online Groups***:* Seek out online communities of like-minded individuals who have faced similar challenges. Share your journey and find support in their collective wisdom. I love the fact that a person can choose to be anonymous online.
- **Trust Your Gut***:* Remember the age-old saying, "If something sounds too good to be true, it probably is." Trust your instincts, and avoid offers that promise quick and easy solutions. Avoid being swayed by tempting but risky propositions. Your financial well-being is more important than any fleeting allure.
- **Don't Follow the Crowd; the Crowd Is Broke***:* Just because everyone around you is going to payday lenders doesn't mean you have to follow suit. Dare to be different! Be the oddball who takes a different path, who chooses financial stability over quick fixes. Prove them wrong and show that there's a smarter, more sustainable way to manage your finances.
- **Become the Wise One***:* You'll become a beacon of wisdom as you acquire knowledge and implement sound financial practices. Others will notice your financial savvy and seek your guidance. Soon, they'll be lining up to learn from your fountain of financial knowledge.

CHAPTER THIRTEEN—CORE LESSONS

- Payday loans are short-term loans designed to provide quick cash until your next payday.
- They often come with extremely high interest rates, making them expensive compared to other types of credit.
- Some borrowers may get trapped in a cycle of debt, taking out new payday loans to cover previous ones.
- If you find yourself in a payday loan cycle, assess your finances and seek assistance from credit counselling agencies or financial advice organisations.

- Explore alternatives to payday loans, such as low-interest personal loans from credit unions or negotiating payment plans with creditors.

Chapter Thirteen—Exercise

If you find yourself using payday lenders, list alternative borrowing options available, such as personal loans, credit union loans, or the Social Fund managed by the Department for Works and Pensions.

Recognise payday loans for what they truly are: predatory lenders targeting vulnerable people. Stay determined to break free from their grasp. Start managing your money with budgets and living within your means so you won't have to rely on short-term cash solutions.

Chapter Fourteen

OVERDRAFTS

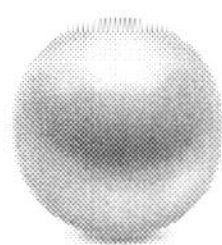

Think of a bank overdraft as borrowing money from your bank when your account balance hits zero or dips below it. For instance, if you have £50 in your account but need to pay a £70 bill, the bank covers that extra £20 if you have an authorised overdraft. Essentially, your bank has permitted you to spend more than what's in your account. However, if you exceed your account balance without this permission, your bank will hit you with penalties, which can be hefty.

I'm not a big fan of overdrafts because, unlike other types of credit, there's no set repayment plan. It tends to just hang around in your account indefinitely, and most banks don't push you to pay it off if you meet their conditions—like regularly depositing your income and not exceeding your authorised overdraft limit.

Many moons ago, I checked my credit score, and it was low. The reason? My current account was always in the red because I was regularly dipping into my overdraft.

Some people are super disciplined. They rarely dip into their overdraft and only use it for emergencies. If this is you, more power to you. Keep your overdraft. But, for some of us mere mortals, the struggle is real. Whenever I could spend more from my account, I always seemed to do so.

I gradually paid off my overdraft, and what do you know? The world did not end when I no longer had an overdraft. I didn't even miss it. So, if you have an overdraft and are always stuck in the red, it might be worth taking proactive steps to get rid of it.

My best argument against having an overdraft is that there is no payoff plan; it just sits on your account year after year. We often go into our overdraft mindlessly, out of habit, and end up constantly in the red.

From a lender's perspective, frequent overdraft use is a sign of poor financial management. Even if your overdraft is authorised by your bank and only a small amount and fee-free, being constantly in the red will show up on your credit report as a negative number and lower your credit score. Anything that lowers your credit score should be avoided.

Here are a few ways to go about it:

1. Gradually reduce your overdraft. I chipped away at mine by £100 each month until it hit zero.
2. Save an amount equal to your overdraft and pay it off in one go.
3. Some people choose to take out a loan to clear their overdraft; just be sure the loan's interest rate is lower than the overdraft's.

The key here is to find the best approach that fits your situation and helps you bid farewell to that overdraft.

CHAPTER FOURTEEN—CORE LESSONS

Understanding Overdrafts

- Overdrafts are borrowing money when your bank account balance hits zero or goes below.
- Overdrafts can be authorised or unauthorised by the bank.
- Authorised overdrafts are permitted by the bank; unauthorised ones incur penalties.

Drawbacks

- There is no set repayment plan.
- Overdrafts can linger indefinitely in your account.
- Regular reliance on your overdraft can harm your credit score.

Managing Overdrafts

- Gradually pay off the overdraft.
- Save and pay it off in one go.
- Consider paying off your overdraft with a lower-interest loan.

Chapter Fifteen

TOO MUCH DEBT—A SYSTEM RIGGED AGAINST YOU

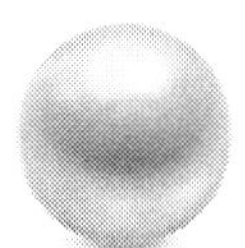

Being over-indebted means having too much debt, like owing more money than you can pay comfortably. It's like being stuck in a situation where debt repayments, take up so much of your income that you either cannot make all the required payments or make the payments at the expense of other essentials like food and other bills. Over-indebtedness can make you feel trapped and overwhelmed.

Sometimes, we become overindebted because we spend more than we earn and rely on debt to cover the gap. But did you know that sometimes, even banks can nudge us toward taking on more debt than we can handle?

Let me share a true story that highlights how banks' relentless pursuit of profit can push even the most responsible customers into financial ruin.

A woman walked into her bank for what she thought was a routine transaction. I was assigned to assist her. She was a familiar face, a loyal customer who had been with us for 18 years. She had a mortgage, some savings, and an impeccable record of managing her finances responsibly. When I entered her details into the system, the screen lit up with various credit offers—credit cards, loans against her property, and more.

In the bank's eyes, this woman was the ideal customer: reliable, stable, and profitable. Because of her excellent history, the bank flooded her with offers she didn't actually need:

A credit card with a £12,000 limit

The option to borrow up to £100,000 extra against her property

A secured loan for £25,000, tied to her property

An unsecured loan for £15,000

As a bank employee, I was duty-bound to inform her of these offers. She was intrigued by the credit card and decided to take it but declined the others. I thought that was the end of it.

But a few days later, she returned, asking to extend her mortgage and take the secured loan. I was puzzled and, out of concern, gently asked why she suddenly needed such significant amounts of money, given that only a week ago she declined all these offers. To my surprise, she got offended and accused me of trying to deny her rights to credit. She even complained to my manager.

My manager was not pleased. He scolded and reminded me that it wasn't my job to discourage borrowing—our branch targets depended on customers taking out loans, and since she was eager to do so, I had no choice but to process the loans. Her monthly debt payments skyrocketed from £355 to £1,516.

Months passed, and then she returned to the bank one day, but this time, she was visibly distressed. She had lost her job, used up all her savings, and was now drowning in debt, and our bank was threatening to repossess her home because she had missed some payments.

As she sat down, she explained what had happened. After taking the credit card, she confided in a close relative back home about the bank's offers. This relative convinced her to take out the loans and invest in a business venture with him. He painted a picture of a golden opportunity that would secure her future. With newfound excitement, she borrowed the extra money and sent the funds to the relative.

But it was all a scam. The relative she trusted had duped her. To try to recover her losses, she frequently travelled to her home country. The stress of these trips, combined with the demands of her job, became too much—she was eventually forced to resign.

The bank made tempting offers that ended up having serious consequences for this customer. Sure, she wasn't forced, but banks prey on our lack of financial knowledge, setting traps we often fall into. The result? Her once stable life unravelled, leaving her jobless, on the verge of homelessness, and struggling with severe health problems.

I wish I could tell you how her story ended, but I left the bank shortly after that incident. But there are countless similar stories where banks lead customers into debt by tempting them with irresistible offers.

Banks have changed a bit since the 2008 crash to avoid pushing customers too hard. But they still spend loads on ads to catch our attention. Since fewer people visit bank branches now, banks use apps and online ads to reel us in. According to The Financial Brand, UK banks are pumping up their marketing budgets to push credit cards and loans (Cocheo, 2024). The Advertising Association/WARC Expenditure Report (2024) says UK ad spending will hit £39.4 billion in 2024, with a big chunk going to financial services, including banks.

You're scrolling through social media, looking at your friends' dazzling holiday photos from exotic locations. Just as envy sets in, an ad pops up and offers you a loan to fund your dream getaway. Banks aren't just guessing—they're tracking your online habits, ready to turn your desires into debt. With one click, that holiday could be yours, and so too could the mounting debt repayments.

MANAGING OVER-INDEBTEDNESS

Signs You Might Be Over-Indebted:

- **Struggling with Minimum Payments:** It's tough to cover just the minimum on your debts.
- **Using Credit for Basics:** Using credit cards or loans for everyday things like groceries or rent.
- **Late or Missed Payments:** Frequently missing or delaying payments.
- **Growing Credit Card Balances:** Credit card debt keeps rising without being paid off monthly.
- **Borrowing to Repay Debts:** Taking new loans to pay off old ones, also known as "robbing Peter to pay Paul."
- **Feeling Overwhelmed:** Constant stress or anxiety about your finances.
- **Avoiding Financial Reality:** Ignoring bills or avoiding discussions about your debt.

If any of these apply to you, seek help. Talking to someone can reduce stress. Consider financial counselling, a debt management program, or negotiating with creditors for flexible payments.

Below is a list of UK organisations that help people deal with debt, along with their website and telephone contact information:

- StepChange Debt Charity Website: https://www.stepchange.org/. Telephone: 0800 138 1111.
- Citizens Advice Website: https://www.citizensadvice.org.uk/. Telephone: Visit the website and enter your postcode for the local Citizens Advice contact details.
- National Debtline Website: https://www.nationaldebtline.org/. Telephone: 0808 808 4000.
- Christians Against Poverty (CAP) Website: https://capuk.org/. Telephone: 0800 328 0006.
- PayPlan Website: https://www.payplan.com/. Telephone: 0800 280 2816.
- Money Advice Service Website: https://www.moneyadviceservice.org.uk/. Telephone: 0800 138 7777.
- StepUp Website: https://www.moneyadviceservice.org.uk/en/tools/stepup. Telephone: Visit the website and enter your postcode for local contact details.
- Debt Advice Foundation Website: https://www.debtadvicefoundation.org/. Telephone: 0800 043 4050.
- MoneysavingExpert Debt Help Website: https://www.moneysavingexpert.com/loans/debt-help-plan/.
- Shelter (for housing-related debt) Website: https://england.shelter.org.uk/. Telephone: Visit the website and enter your postcode for local contact details.

Please note that telephone numbers and website addresses may change, so it's always a good idea to double-check the contact details on their websites.

PRACTICAL STRATEGIES FOR DEBT REDUCTION

While the listed organisations can help you out temporarily, but lasting change needs your effort. I shared how I tackled my debt through simple budgetting and cautious spending. This helped me find lasting financial stability, and I hope to help you find the same peace and freedom.

This section explores practical strategies for managing debt. We'll cover popular methods such as Snowball, Avalanche, and Balance Transfer. These methods are effective for managing multiple debts.

Snowball Strategy

The snowball method focuses on paying off your smallest debt first, regardless of the interest rate. Then, you move on to the next smallest debt and continue until every debt is paid off.

Here's how it works:

- List your debts from smallest to largest outstanding balance.
- Make minimum payments on all listed debts.
- Put any extra money you can toward paying off the smallest debt, which should be at the top of your list.
- Once the smallest debt is paid off, roll over the payment to the next debt on your list.
- Keep repeating this process, paying off one debt at a time and rolling over the payments to the next debt.

Using my debt as an example, here is what a snowball debt repayment strategy looks like:

Debts	My Starting Balances	My Minimum Payment	Additional Payment	Total Monthly Payments	Debt Paid Off in the
Post Office Credit Card	£900	£27	£300	£327	3rd month
Barclaycard	£6,000	£180	£327 (from Post Office)	£507	17th month
MBNA Credit Card	£9,000	£270	£507 (from Barclaycard)	£777	26th month
Halifax Credit Card	£11,000	£330	£777 (from MBNA)	£1,107	32nd month

After reducing all my expenses and finding ways to boost my income, I freed up an additional £300 to pay down my credit card debts.

The snowball method is popular because it gives a quick win. I paid off the first card in three months, so I have only three credit cards to worry about. It felt good—finally, I was making progress.

Avalanche Strategy

The avalanche method is similar to the snowball method, but instead of focusing on paying off the lowest balance first, the priority is paying off the highest-interest debt. An avalanche debt repayment plan will look like this:

Debt	Starting Balance	Interest Rate	Minimum Payment	Additional Payment	Total Monthly Payment	Debt Paid Off in the
Barclaycard	£6,000	27%	£180	£327 (initial additional payment)	£507	15th month
Halifax Credit Card	£11,000	21%	£330	£507 (from Barclaycard)	£837	27th month
MBNA Credit Card	£9,000	19%	£270	£837 (from Halifax)	£1,107	32nd month
Post Office Credit Card	£900	18%	£27	£1,107 (from MBNA)	£1,134	32nd month

Snowball Versus Avalanche

The avalanche method saves you more money on interest payments, but it may take longer to see tangible results compared to the snowball method. With the snowball, the first card was paid off within three months, but with the avalanche, the first card was paid off in fifteen months. It takes dedication, especially at the start of a debt repayment journey. Interest saving between the two methods wasn't astronomical, but a penny saved is a penny earned. The difference in total interest paid is £225. The method you choose depends on whether you need quick wins to keep you motivated or if you can knuckle down and keep your focus even when the process seems long. You can also mix and match. I started with the snowball, then moved on to other methods, as you would soon see.

Balance Transfers

My introduction to balance transfer credit cards was pure luck, but it was a much-needed breakthrough in my debt repayment journey. After successfully paying off the Post Office credit card using the snowball method, I received a letter from the Post Office. They congratulated me on clearing my balance and invited me to transfer other existing debts to their card at a 0% interest rate. At that point, I had three credit cards with high interest rates.

Debt	Balance	Interest Rate	Interest Payment
Barclaycard	£6,000	27%	£135
Halifax Credit Card	£11,000	21%	£192
MBNA Credit Card	£9,000	19%	£142

My Barclaycard had a balance of £6,000. The interest rate was astronomical at 27%. I was shelling out £135 each month in interest, essentially throwing money down the drain because it was not clearing my debt.

Transferring my balance to the Post Office reduced my monthly interest payment from £135 to £0, meaning every penny I now paid into this debt cleared the balance.

This balance transfer scenario played out repeatedly throughout my debt repayment journey. As soon as I transferred my balance from Barclaycard to the Post Office, Barclaycard invited me to transfer other balances back to them. Within six months, all three remaining credit cards were on 0% deals, which saved me £469 monthly.

You might wonder, "How are banks making money when offering a 0% interest rate?" It's a valid question because banks are in the business of making a profit. Banks charge a **balance transfer fee**.

Before you accept a balance transfer deal, crunch the numbers and ensure the transfer fee isn't higher than the interest you'd pay on the card you're transferring from. The balance transfer fee charged by the Post Office was lower than the monthly interest rate I was paying to Barclaycard. When the numbers add up in your favour, a balance transfer is an excellent way to control your debt.

There is another sneaky way banks try to make money on balance transfers. The Post Office hopes that once the 0% deal ends, I'll go back to not paying off my credit card in full monthly, and then they can resume charging interest. How do they know this? Well, they've been keeping an eye on my financial habits. They know my spending patterns and history. In the past, I had never fully paid off my monthly balance, and they were certainly not ready to let me off the hook that easily. So, they offered me a balance transfer deal, probably thinking, "Joyce is likely to go back to her old habit of not fully clearing her credit card balance. When the 0% deal ends, we can start charging her interest again." However, little did they know that I had become financially "woke" and was determined never to pay a single penny in interest. I made it my mission to clear all balances within the deal period and succeeded.

The avalanche method became irrelevant since high interest rates were no longer an issue. My priority shifted to paying off the debt with the shortest 0% period, as shown below. It was now a race against time.

Balance Transfer Deal	0% Deal
1st Post Office	12-Months
2nd Barclaycard	18-Months
3rd MBNA Card	36-Months

Stay one step ahead, and do not fall into the interest trap when these deals end. Set up the deal end dates in your calendar with a three-month reminder; that way, if you cannot pay off the balance in time, you can seek alternative methods to pay off the balance as cheaply as possible.

If you have multiple credit cards that you are trying to pay off and your credit rating is still good, balance transfers are a helpful tool in your debt repayment toolbox.

Securing Balance Transfer Deals

Getting Balance Transfer deals is straightforward.

- Consistently paying down your debts improves your credit rating, which catches your bank's attention. As a result, they might offer you a balance transfer deal.
- A proactive approach is to actively seek balance transfer deals but be mindful of the impact multiple credit applications in a short period can have on your credit score.

DEBT CONSOLIDATION LOANS

In a previous chapter, we touched on debt consolidation loans, but let's recap. Debt consolidation loans simplify debt management by combining multiple debts into one loan with a lower interest rate. They also provide an opportunity to negotiate better terms.

However, a challenge with this method is that some may repay their credit cards with the loan but then continue to use their credit cards. This undermines the purpose of debt consolidation.

Another drawback of debt consolidation loans is that loans often have fixed payments, making it difficult to make extra payments and clear the debt as quickly as possible.

Making Debt Consolidation Work

To ensure the success of your debt consolidation effort, consider the following:

- Cut up your credit cards so you don't go shopping with them and run up more debt.
- Remove credit card information from all online shopping sites to prevent easy spending.
- Cancel credit cards altogether if you are still tempted to spend on them.
- Look for consolidation loans with flexible options that allow for overpayments when you have extra cash.
- Develop a mindset that says no to consumer debt and yes to saving for what you want.

DEVELOPING A DEBT-FREE MINDSET

I grew up in a place where debt was uncommon. The most expensive purchase individuals make is their homes, but even that was never purchased with debt. In most of Africa, you'd save up to buy a piece of land, then save up again to build your home little by little until it was completed.

Coming to the UK, I remember how scared I was for a friend when she took out a £40,000 mortgage to buy her home. I lay awake worrying for her, "All that money to pay for 25 years, what if she loses her job?". At that time, I had a debt-free mindset. Using debt for any kind of purchase was an alien concept and scared me. But, with time, my mindset gradually shifted. I became accustomed to living with debt. Buying homes, cars, furniture, and even clothes on credit became normal. Saving money is a good habit but hard and takes time; why save when loans are available to immediately give me what I want? In essence, I went from having a "no-debt mindset" to a "debt is not so bad" mindset. I ended up owning thousands as a result of this mind shift.

What I needed was a balanced view of debt. Now, my opinion of debt is that it is a necessary evil. It is necessary only for enhancements that generate future assets—enhancements that would be a home, an education, and business loans. Anything outside these, debt is a big no.

Developing a debt-free mindset means I rethink my approach to borrowing. Gone are the days when I thought all debts were evil or that debt was normal. If I had all the money in the world to fund major capital purchases and business expansions, I would never touch debt again. I cannot make that claim yet, so I might touch debt in the future for capital purchases or funding a business. The difference in my approach to debt now lies in its use—as a tool to make more money only.

For-sale signs hold no appeal to me. I am not bothered that my phone is five years old as long as it performs its basic functions. I am super content with my little possessions. Especially knowing that discontent is usually rooted in deeper stuff. Shopping for me was plastering a festering wound. So, if I ever feel discontent, unhappy, or fear missing out on some great adventure, I dig deeper into the feeling side of my equation and find ways to fix this discontentment. Rather than buy more stuff that leaves me broke and feeling hollow.

This is my debt story. What is yours? If you grew up in the Western world, debt might seem normal. Think back to all those catalogues of yesteryear—the Littlewoods of the past, now replaced with online shops inviting us to buy £10 clothing on credit. Debt might seem normal, but it is not. Debt is convenient. But we pay a heavy price for this convenience. Perhaps the most egregious thing debt has done is diminish the excellent financial habit of saving.

We must return to good habits like saving and investing. If saving feels tough, revisit the chapter on budgeting. Imagine saving and spending as two boxers in the ring. **Drumroll, pleas**e! In the blue corner, we have the heavyweight champion—**Super Saver**! And in the red corner, the reigning champion—**Super Spender**! You must pick which fighter you want to back in this money match. So, who will be the winner in your financial story?

CHAPTER FIFTEEN—CORE LESSONS

- Debt can trap you—too much debt overwhelms your finances and your life.
- Banks are profit-driven: They often push credit and loans, tempting us with offers that can quickly spiral into financial trouble.
- Use proven debt repayment methods such as snowball, avalanche or balance transfers to regain control of your finances.

- Help is available. Organisations like StepChange, Citizens Advice, and National Debtline in the UK are ready to help you manage debt.
- Change how you view debt. Start seeing debt as something only to be used for creating value—like buying a home, getting an education, or investing in a business.
- Prioritise saving over borrowing: Debt discourages the habit of saving. Focus on building better habits like saving and investing for the future.

Chapter Fifteen—Exercise

1. List your debts and the total amount owed.
2. Revisit your budget and calculate your leftover money after paying essential expenses.
3. Can you afford to pay more than the minimum debt payments? If not, reassess and explore ways to trim expenses in other areas so you can allocate more money towards debt repayment.
4. Be relentless in your quest to be free of high-interest debt. Take steps to increase your payments to reduce debts, as this is crucial for breaking free from debt and achieving financial freedom.

Chapter Sixteen

SAVE AND BUILD WEALTH—ONE POUND AT A TIME

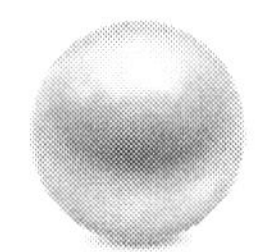

In writing this book, I embarked on a quest to uncover savings secrets. I even sought the wisdom of a five-year-old prodigy named Matthew, who was quite the financial philosopher. I asked him if he saved any of his pocket money, and, to my surprise, he said no. But when I questioned whether saving was good, he replied with a resounding yes.

Naturally, I probed further, asking why he didn't save despite knowing it was a good idea. His response was priceless: "There's just too many cool sweets to buy!"

However, he did mention his friend Josh, who never splurged on sweets but saved every penny to buy the coolest toys. And guess what? Josh recently bought a mind-blowing "Technic Monster Jam" with his hard-earned savings. I must admit, I had to google what that was (it turns out it's a Lego truck), but Matthew spelling out the benefits of delaying gratification left me in awe! By saving and not giving in to the impulse to buy sweets, Josh could get something nice that he can play with for longer.

Now, let's be real here. Saving money may not be the most exhilarating topic, but it's crucial for financial success. I don't want to waste your time or bore you with obvious advice. We all know saving is good. But if you need extra convincing, just seek out the Matthews in your life—they'll set you straight.

Instead, let's embark on a thrilling adventure and unravel why we find it hard to save. It's time to dig deep, unearth the reasons, and discover practical solutions that will transform our saving habits. Get ready because this chapter will take you on an enchanting, entertaining, and enlightening journey that will make saving as exciting as a Technic Monster Jam. Okay, maybe not that exciting … but I promise you, saving is more fascinating than you think.

Before we continue, let me assure you that my research on savings went far beyond conversations with five-year-olds. I've explored the minds of a diverse range of individuals, seeking to unravel why saving seems challenging for so many.

My findings? Well, 70% of respondents blame insufficient income for their savings struggles. They're just trying to make ends meet, and once all essentials are paid, there is nothing left to save.

Then we have the 5% who face emergencies that constantly drain their savings, leaving them feeling like they're "back to square one." Only 10% attribute their non-saving habit to a lack of financial know-how.

Ten per cent of grown-ups admit they're like our little Matthew, who can't resist buying things on a whim. They just can't say no when they see something on sale. Another 5% think that their family, religion, or culture affects how good they are at saving money.

I think many of us don't save because we've bought into the idea that it's just too hard to save, and everybody is in the same non-saving boat. *"And, if I can't beat them, I might as well join them."* I do agree. Saving is hard. It is hard because saving comes down to making choices—saying no to what we want. It's hard to say no to ourselves, especially if we think society is constantly saying no to us. Saving money has never been easy. In fact, it was tougher for people like my parents in the '50s and '60s. They earned super low wages from menial jobs, yet they still managed to save. Back then, saving was the norm because there weren't convenient alternatives like credit cards or loans to rely on in emergencies.

There's an old Yoruba saying, "We can't eat with all ten fingers," meaning we can't spend everything we earn. This mindset was deeply ingrained—spending all your money without setting some aside for savings was not normal.

Recently, my mum told me about the flats they lived in the '60s and how they chose not to heat the whole flat just to save money. They willingly gave up some comfort so they could put money aside. I'm not saying we need to live like that today, but it makes you think: if they could sacrifice that much just to save, what are we willing to give up to build our savings now?

How we live our lives shouldn't be determined by society, our friends, or our family—it should be shaped by our income and personal goals. We often compare ourselves to others and try to keep up with what we think is the ideal lifestyle. But if we focus instead on our income, our expenses, and the savings we want to achieve, our lifestyle choices will look different.

HOW DO WE BECOME SAVERS?

Every transformation begins in one's thoughts. We must accept that setting aside a portion of our income for savings is the norm rather than the exception. We should feel uncomfortable if we spend all our income and maybe more on credit. Earning and spending it all is not the way to go. If we live this way, we must recognise that change is needed to rectify this anomaly.

- **Pay yourself first:** Every expense is paying someone else. Saving is paying yourself. You work hard for your money, so why won't you pay yourself first? Make savings a priority by dedicating the top line in your budget to savings. Saving should never be an afterthought; it deserves the spotlight.
- **You need a budget**: Track every single penny that comes and goes. No more mental arithmetic or quick maths. A budget eliminates the guesswork.
- **Trim the fat**: Identify those non-essential expenses and mercilessly eliminate them. Look at every discretionary item you spend your money on and ask yourself, who deserves my money more than me? Just Eat, Amazon, or the Afro Hair and Beauty store?
- **Bargain with the forces of essential bills and expenses.** Take the time to negotiate and shop around for better deals on bills and all recurring expenses. Any savings you make should be diverted to your savings accounts.
- **Cultivate a saving habit**. Saving is a habit. Even if it's just a humble £1 per month, get into the habit of saving consistently. Start small and forge a steadfast, iron-clad saving routine.
- **Keep your savings sacred**. Maintain a separate account for your savings, potentially at a different bank, far away from your spending money. Don't treat your savings account as an extension of your current account. Avoid logging in too frequently. Let those savings grow quietly in the background.
- **Keep it saved**. Once you've saved your hard-earned money, resist the urge to dip into it.
- **Enlist the aid of automation.** Set up automatic transfers from your current account to your savings account. By automating your savings, you'll ensure a portion of your income is consistently allocated towards saving before you can spend it elsewhere.
- **Oops, a slip-up? No worries!** If you occasionally succumb to the temptation and withdraw from your savings, don't beat yourself up

about it. Tomorrow is another day, another chance to embrace the saving spirit. I slipped up so many times before I finally stopped dipping into my savings.

- **Set achievable savings goals**. Establish specific and realistic savings goals that you can work towards. Whether saving for an emergency fund, a deposit to buy your home, having those clear, SMART goals will keep you motivated and focused on your saving journey. The bank I save with allows personalised savings spaces where you define your goals. It helps me visualise my progress as I add to my savings.

WHAT SHOULD YOU SAVE FOR FIRST?

Knowing what to start saving for is important. I am sure the order of what to save for will be no surprise. I have spoken on these throughout this book. The key is to keep it super simple. Let's not be that person who goes from having no savings to having ten different savings accounts.

Priority 1: Emergency Fund

Building an emergency fund should be your top priority. It is a financial safety net. We cannot predict the future, but we can prepare ourselves for unexpected situations like job loss or other unforeseen expenses. Aim to have three to six months' worth of living expenses saved up.

Emergency Funds and Debt: Balancing Priorities

If you have high-interest debt like credit cards, personal loans, payday loans, or store cards, the general rule is to pay off this debt before saving. I've seen people proudly show off £5,000 in savings while still owing over £10,000 in credit card debt. The problem is that the interest you pay on debt is usually much higher than what you earn on savings. A person with £5,000 in savings but £10,000 in credit card debt has a negative net worth of £5,000.

Pay down high-interest debts, then focus on building your savings. Having some money set aside for emergencies while paying down debt is important. Aim to save £500 to £1,000 as a basic emergency fund. After that, work on paying down your debt. Once your debts are gone, fully fund your emergency savings to cover three to six months of living expenses. This balanced approach prepares you for emergencies and lets you pay off your debt simultaneously.

Priority 2: Short-Term Goals

After sorting your emergency fund, focus on saving for short-term goals. Whether saving a deposit to buy your dream home, a wedding, a dream vacation, a gadget, or a car. Saving for these goals helps you avoid taking on debt.

Priority 3: Investing in Long-Term Goals

Once we've saved for emergencies and other short-term goals, it's time to start thinking about investing. Investing has the potential for much higher growth than just saving in a deposit account.

SAVING OR INVESTING, WHICH IS BETTER?

Saving and investing are both important financial habits that we should all have. Saving is storing your money in a safe place like your bank. You can access it with no fuss when you need it, and there is no risk of losing your money. However, the interest rates for savings are typically low. We should all start with savings and move into investing once all short-term needs are taken care of.

Investing is putting your money to work to earn more money. The earning potential is higher, but so is the risk of losing money. Investing focuses more on the long term, which helps build wealth.

An example is the best way to explain the difference between investing and saving.

Two people who are both good with money. One person saves monthly in a regular savings account that pays 4% interest, while the other chooses to invest it in an index fund, like the S&P 500. They both invest £250 monthly for ten years. The table below shows their results.

Scenario	Monthly Contribution	Account Type	Interest/ Return Rate	Total Invested	Growth/ Interest Earned	Total Amount After 10 Years
Saver	£250	Regular Saver Account	4% Interest	£30,000	£6,812	£36,812
Investor	£250	Index Fund (S&P 500)	10% Return	£30,000	£21,000	£51,000

The investor made more money. While investing doesn't guarantee you'll always make a profit, and past results don't promise future profits, the average annual return for indexes like the S&P 500 has been around 10% (Maverick, 2024).

I mentioned index funds earlier, but here's a quick reminder: An index fund lets you invest in many companies at once. For example, the S&P 500 includes 500 top US companies, while the FTSE 250 covers 250 companies in the UK. When you invest in an index fund, you buy a small piece of all these companies. As the companies grow, so does the money you invest in them. Index funds usually have low fees, and investing in them is straightforward—almost as easy as saving in a bank account.

That said, investing in index funds does have risks—you can lose money. But they're considered less risky than other investments because your money is spread across many companies. This makes index funds a safer option for long-term investing.

If there's one thing I want you to takeaway, it's this, saving and investing are both important, but they serve different purposes. We should be doing both. Usually, it's best to start with saving and then move into investing.

Investing is much like saving. Just as you choose a bank for your savings, you choose an investment company for your investments. You decide where to put your money—like in an index fund or other investments—and then set up regular payments from your bank account. The investment company handles the rest.

Before I knew about investing, I imagined it as a noisy, chaotic room with traders shouting and screens flashing. It seemed confusing, so I stayed away. But investing is actually quite simple. You just deposit money into your investment account and check it every so often. I look at mine every six months.

OTHER INVESTMENT TYPES

Stocks: Buying shares in a company. They are considered high-risk should the company fail, but can have big rewards.

Bonds: Lending money to a company or government and earning interest. These are considered lower risk but with smaller returns.

Mutual Funds: Mutual funds are similar to index funds. Their investments are managed by experts and include a mix of stocks and bonds.

Real Estate: involves buying properties to rent or sell for profit. It's simple but requires a lot of money upfront. Rent can provide a steady income.

REITs (Real Estate Investment Trusts): Investing in companies that own real estate without buying property yourself.

Commodities: Investing in things like gold or oil. Helps protect against inflation.

Cryptocurrency: Digital money like Bitcoin. Very risky but can offer big returns.

P2P Lending: Lending money to people or businesses through online platforms and earning interest.

Crowdfunding/Startups: Investing small amounts in new companies for a share of the profits. This is a high-risk investment, as the majority of Startups fail.

The financial landscape changes quickly, so it's always a good idea to do some research when selecting savings accounts. An effective approach is to search online for specific types of accounts that suit your needs. For example, if you're looking for an account for your emergency funds, simply type "instant access savings accounts" into your search engine. Look for reputable brands and ensure they are regulated in the UK.

To wrap things up, saving and investing are essential for financial success. Saving is storing money for short-term needs. Spending everything we earn without saving is not normal—saving is paying ourselves, while spending is paying everybody else. You might need to cut back on non-essential expenses to make room for saving. Once you've saved enough for your short-term goals, shift your attention to investing. Investing helps your money grow over the long term and gives you a better chance of building wealth.

CHAPTER SIXTEEN—CORE LESSONS

- Saving is storing money for our short-term needs like emergencies and big purchases.
- Spending all our income without saving is abnormal.
- Saving is paying ourselves first, while spending is paying others.
- To save more, we need to cut back on unnecessary expenses.
- Once we've saved for short-term goals, it's time to focus on investing for long-term growth.
- While riskier than saving, investing can grow our money and build wealth over time.
- Index funds are a simple and less risky way to start investing. They spread your money across many companies and have lower fees.
- Both saving and investing are important. Start by saving, then move on to investing when you're ready.
- Set up regular payments into your savings or investment account and check in occasionally.

Chapter Sixteen—Exercise

If you are new to saving:

1. Start with a small achievable goal. £100 or £500 is ideal. If you can save more, go for it.
2. Write down your monthly income and every penny you spend for one month, and look for areas where you can cut back.
3. Set aside any savings from your expense-cutting exercise.
4. If you don't have one, open a separate account for your savings.
5. Set up automatic transfers into your savings account, starting with a small amount.
6. Keep saving regularly. The habit is more important than the amount saved.
7. Track your progress every three months.

If you already save but want to start investing:

- Make your first investment with £50 or £100. This small step will help you become comfortable with investing.
- Read up on simple investment options like index funds or ETFs. These are beginner-friendly and easy to understand.
- Choose a beginner-friendly platform with low fees. Here are three popular options:
    1. **Nutmeg**: A user-friendly platform with managed portfolios and automated options.
    2. **Hargreaves Lansdown**: Offers a wide range of investments, helpful tools, and strong customer support.
    3. **Vanguard**: Known for its low-cost index funds and ETFs, ideal for beginners.
- Put your first £50 or £100 into an index fund or ETF on your chosen platform.
- Don't check your investment daily. Investing is long-term, so review your progress every 3-6 months.
- As you gain confidence, gradually expand your knowledge and consider additional investments.

Chapter Seventeen

SAVING FOR RETIREMENT

When I was pregnant with my first child, I saw a newspaper headline that rattled me. It claimed raising a child from birth to age 12 would cost no less than £500,000. At the time, I didn't have a thousand pounds, let alone hundreds of thousands.

Worrying about not having £500,000 felt pointless and out of my control. What I could control was loving and protecting my child. So, I soon forgot about that headline and focused on what mattered. I ended up raising two well-loved, well-rounded, upright citizens. I didn't need a million pounds to do it, and they turned out just fine.

The point? We can't believe everything we read in newspapers, even the so-called reputable ones.

IGNORE THE HYPE; FOCUS ON THE MISSION

Much of the talk around retirement savings feels like that £500,000 headline. We're bombarded with messages saying no one is saving enough for retirement and that we all need a million pounds to live comfortably. But I often wonder about the people writing these headlines—they must live in a different world. For them, maybe it does take half a million to raise a child or retire comfortably. The problem is they make it sound like everyone needs these huge amounts, which can feel overwhelming. For many people, saving £1,000 is tough. So, when they read that they need millions to retire, it can seem impossible and may even make them give up on saving altogether.

If the hype around retirement savings has discouraged or depressed you, I invite you to tune it out. This book is about building wealth for yourself, your children, and future generations. Retirement is a big part of that. And right now, our community is struggling. The danger of doing nothing is that we risk poverty in old age, more reliance on the Black tax, and passing on poverty to the next generation. So, ignore the noise and focus on the mission: building a retirement fund that will support you and benefit those who come after you.

"We are built to last. Black women live the longest"
(Office for National Statistics, 2021)

I don't know anyone who prays to die young. We all pray to live long, healthy lives. Well, sisters, our prayers are answered. In the UK, Black women have the longest life expectancy—Black African women live up to 88.9 years compared to the average lifespan of 85.8 years.

Wouldn't it be wonderful to use those extra years to do the things we love? Travelling, spending time with family, enjoying hobbies, volunteering, and savouring life's simple pleasures. All of this is within reach. But we need to think about how we will fund these dreams.

With longer lives comes the need for stronger retirement planning. After all, living longer without enough money only means more years of struggle. So, what's your plan for those 24 or more years in retirement? How will you ensure you have enough to live on once you stop working?

There are already worrying trends. Research from Scottish Widows shows that Black women face significant challenges regarding retirement planning (Scottish Widows, 2021).

- **30% of Black women** plan to continue working part-time instead of fully retiring because they feel they can't afford a comfortable retirement.
- **More than half of Black women (52%)** who have some retirement savings are concerned about running out of money in retirement.
- **Almost one in six Black women (14%)** are opting out of pension schemes altogether. They don't trust the system or feel they can't afford to save.

After everything we've worked for, do we really want to keep working when we should be enjoying the fruits of our labour? Let's do everything we can to beat this trend. It's never too late. With some planning, we can all look forward to a fulfilling retirement.

THE STRUGGLE TO PICTURE OUR FUTURE SELVES

The reasons we struggle with saving for retirement is that we can't picture older versions of ourselves. And, we're so overwhelmed by day-to-day expenses that we push thoughts of the future out of our minds. I've been there.

During my worst financial struggles, my coping mechanism was to get through each day. "Just help me get through today", I'd pray. Retirement savings or any kind of forward planning was not on my radar. So, I understand the struggle. The Netflix documentary "*Get Smart With Money*" reveals that to most, the future feels distant, almost unreal. So, we don't prioritise long-term savings. We're stuck in the moment, trying to meet immediate needs.

The good news is that as we apply the principles we've learned throughout this book, our finances will improve—mine did.

When our finances are messy, and we don't have enough money to meet our needs, it can feel like being stuck in the worst traffic jam. You can't move forward; you can't go backwards or turn sideways. It feels like there is no way out. Everything feels frustrating. But as you nip here and tuck there, things start to free up. The same applies to your finances. As you make small adjustments here and there, you start to free up cash, allowing you to do more than you ever thought possible.

This is how to approach retirement savings. By following the steps we've discussed, you'll create the financial space to invest in your future. And it's crucial—because if managing money is hard now, think about how much tougher it could get when we're older and our earning options are fewer. We cannot afford to ignore our future selves.

Now that we've identified the importance of planning for our future, let's get practical. It's all well and good to avoid the noise, but we still need a solid game plan in place. While the headlines might seem overwhelming, breaking things down into simple, actionable steps is the way to go. Just as you've started taking control of your finances throughout this book, planning for retirement is another key area where small, steady actions today can lead to big rewards tomorrow.

The first question usually on everyone's mind is, "How much should I actually be saving?" Let's tackle that million-dollar question by examining the factors shaping our retirement needs.

HOW MUCH SHOULD I BE SAVING FOR?

The general rule of thumb is that you'll need about two-thirds of your pre-retirement income to live on after you retire. For example, if you are earning £30,000 a year now, you'll need around £20,000 for retirement. The reduced amounts assume a few things. You won't need to travel to work every day, which removes transport costs. You won't need work clothes. You won't have rent or mortgage payments if you own your property outright. But, as everyone's situation is different, let's approach this from another angle by asking ourselves these four key questions?

What lifestyle do I want in retirement?

- **Basic:** Essentials covered with a little extra for fun.
- **Moderate:** Essentials covered with more security and flexibility.
- **Comfortable:** Essentials covered with full financial freedom and luxury

What will my expenses look like based on my lifestyle choice?

I found a great website called Retirement Living Standards. It helps you picture your ideal retirement by breaking down costs like housing, travel, and food for different lifestyles. It's worth checking out to get an idea of what your living costs might be. Visit it at www.retirementlivingstandards.org.uk. You'll have a rough idea of your retirement expenses by the end.

How Much Money Do I Already Have for Retirement?

State Pension: Paid by the UK government once you reach retirement age (currently 66, but this may rise). The amount you get is currently about £221.20 per week (around £950 per month). You must make 35 years of National Insurance contributions to get the full state pension. Use the Check Your State Pension Forecast service on GOV.UK to estimate your future pension.

Workplace Pensions: If you've been employed, your employer may have offered a workplace pension, in which you and the employer contributed to your retirement savings.

Contact your previous employers for details about the pension schemes you were enrolled in. If unsure, use the Pension Tracing Service on GOV.UK to track them down. Request up-to-date statements from each provider to see your current pot size and projected income.

Private Pensions, Savings, and Investments: Get current statements for any private or stakeholder pensions. Review all savings and investments (ISAs, savings accounts, etc.).

Once you've gathered all possible retirement savings, use online tools like the MoneyHelper Pension Calculator to estimate your total retirement income. These tools can help you project how much you'll have based on current savings and expected growth.

Is there a gap between my retirement income and expenses?

Thanks to online calculators, you should now have an idea of your expected retirement expenses and an estimate of your income. If you have a surplus and can live comfortably, then hurrah! You can look forward to retirement with ease. But if there is a gap, don't panic. Identify the shortfall—chances are, it's not millions of pounds.

CLOSING THE PENSION GAP

If you find a gap between your retirement income and your expected needs, don't worry—you have options. The sooner you act, the more flexibility you'll have. Focus on these two core strategies: increase your income and reduce your expenses. By doing both, you'll close the gap faster.

Maximising all available retirement-saving options is a good way to close that gap. Here's an overview of the most common retirement saving schemes and how they can benefit you.

Defined Contribution Pension Schemes

Think of a Defined Contribution pension as a pot. You and your employer contribute a percentage of your salary, and the government adds tax relief. The money is invested and grows over time. The earlier you start, the bigger the pot.

One key point: if you don't contribute, neither does your employer. That's free money you're missing out on! If you're not in your employer's pension scheme, now's the time to join. Visit HR, tell them you've changed your mind, and start saving for your future. Auto-enrolment makes it easy—deductions happen automatically from your salary, meaning you save effortlessly. You can increase your contributions as your income grows. Your retirement savings plan can also move with you if you change jobs.

If you earn less than £10,000 or are under 22, which is the minimum age for auto-enrolment, you can still opt into your employer's retirement savings plan. While your employer can't automatically enrol you, you have the right to join. Many people don't know this, so it's worth asking.

Defined Benefit Pension Schemes

A Defined Benefit plan gives you a guaranteed income for life based on your final salary and how long you've worked with the company. These plans aren't offered to new members anymore, but you might still have one if you've worked for a big company or in the public sector.

Personal Pension Schemes

Being your own boss is great, but it has some drawbacks—especially in retirement planning. Auto-enrolment doesn't apply to the self-employed, which leaves many self-employed individuals without proper retirement savings. As Black women in the UK increasingly become self-employed, we must prioritise our future selves. Private pension schemes also work for employees who may want to save over and above their employer's pension plan.

Here are some options:

- **Personal Pensions**: Providers like Aviva or PensionBee make it easy to set up.
- **SIPP**: Offers control over your investments if you want to manage them yourself.
- **NEST**: A low-cost, government-backed option for simplicity.
- **Stakeholder Pensions**: Flexible contributions with low fees

One final note—if you're self-employed, your business could be a powerful income stream in retirement. Could you explore automating parts of your business using technology or outsourcing to generate passive income? Now is a good time to start thinking about turning your business into an automatic income-generating machine.

GETTING A PENSION IF YOU'RE UNEMPLOYED

Being out of work or taking time off to care for family can affect your pension savings. But you can still build up your State Pension through national insurance credits. If you're getting Child Benefits, Carer's Allowance, or certain unemployment benefits, these credits help cover the gaps in your contributions. To check if you've got enough credits, just head over to the *Check Your State Pension* service on the GOV.UK website.

MAKING UP FOR LOST TIME

It's never too late to start saving. Even if you're in your 40s, 50s or 60s and worried you haven't saved enough, there's still time to act. Consider increasing your contributions to your workplace or personal retirement plan. Every pound you save today can make a significant difference in your future. Let's look at an example:

Meet Adi and Yemi, two friends who started working at the same company. Both joined the company's retirement plan, where for every pound they contribute, their employer adds 50p.

Adi signed up for the retirement plan as soon as he started working. On the other hand, Yemi had too many financial obligations at the time and felt he couldn't afford to save for his retirement. It took a while, but eventually, Yemi's financial situation improved. Knowing he had to catch up, he decided to go all in on his retirement savings, giving himself about ten years to build his pot.

The table below highlights their different saving strategies and results.

	Adi	Yemi
Monthly Contribution	£100 (started at 22 years old)	£400 (started at 50 years old)
Contribution Period	40 years	10 years
Adi's/Yemi's Contribution	£48,000	£48,000
Employer Contribution	£24,000	£24,000
Total Contributions	£72,000	£72,000
Rate of Return (at 7%)	£393,000	£88,000

Moral of the story? Actually, there are two:

1. **Start as early as possible.** Don't wait until you're earning big money—starting small can make a huge difference. The secret is compounding interest, which helps your savings grow faster. The money you save earns interest, and then that interest earns more interest. Over time, even small amounts can turn into something big. That's why time is your best friend when it comes to retirement savings. If you're in your twenties and haven't joined your

employer's plan yet, do it now. The earlier you start, the less you'll need to save later because your money will have more time to grow.

2. **It's never too late to begin.** Yemi may not have as much as Adi, but he still walks away with nearly £90,000. That's a huge win, especially considering the average pension pot for Black African households is just £11,700 (Office for National Statistics, 2020). Starting late is better than not starting at all.

If you're no longer in your 20s or 30s, don't fret—just start now. You may need to save aggressively, but saving something is always better than nothing. Even £10,000 in your retirement pot is better than zero. And remember, any money you save in your workplace or private plan will be on top of your state pension.

OTHER WAYS TO RETIRE COMFORTABLY

Delay Retirement

Delaying retirement gives you more time to save and grows your savings. It also reduces the years you'll need to draw from your retirement savings.

Create Extra Income in Retirement

By retirement, you've built valuable expertise that others are willing to pay for. Why not turn that knowledge into a source of passive income? Digital products like eBooks, courses, or art can generate steady income with low upfront costs. They're scalable, flexible, and can reach a global audience through platforms like Amazon and Udemy. Once set up, these products earn money with minimal effort, letting you build wealth while enjoying your retirement.

Part-time or freelance work is a fulfilling option for those who prefer staying active. Many retirees continue working to stay engaged and purposeful—the extra cash is a bonus.

Reduce Expenses and Cultivate Good Financial Habits

Retiring comfortably isn't about having millions in the bank—it's about covering your expenses with income from independent sources, like your investments. The fewer your expenses, the easier it is to retire comfortably. Start now; don't wait until retirement to simplify your life and cut unnecessary costs. For some, housing remains a major cost. This is another reason we must aim to own our homes and be mortgage-free by retirement. A mortgage-free home drastically reduces your expenses. According to the Joseph Rowntree Foundation, renting pensioners are twice as likely to live in poverty as mortgage-free homeowners.

Good financial habits stack up over time. Paying off your mortgage earlier than scheduled helps you divert funds to your retirement savings and means fewer expenses when retired.

Consider Retirement Abroad

Retiring abroad might be a beautiful option if you rely solely on the UK state pension or don't have much saved up for retirement. The pound stretches further in other parts of the globe, even exotic ones. Countries like Portugal, Spain, Thailand, and Jamaica offer lower living costs, safety, and good healthcare.

Before moving, research visa requirements, healthcare, living costs, and safety. Consult financial and legal advisors to ensure a smooth transition.

- **Safety**: Research the security of your chosen destination.

- **Healthcare**: Ensure adequate medical facilities are available and consider international health insurance.
- **Community**: Look for expatriate communities for support.
- **Legal Requirements**: Check visa requirements for long-term stays. Some countries offer special retirement visas.

Caring for Your Health

As we age, health becomes a priority. Embracing a healthy lifestyle now will not only improve your retirement years but also lower future healthcare costs. After working hard most of your life, staying healthy will allow you to make the most of your well-earned free time.

CONSOLIDATING PENSIONS FROM MULTIPLE JOBS

If you've worked for multiple employers and forgotten the details of any pension pots, the free **Pension Tracing Service** can help you track them down. This government service locates lost or forgotten pensions in the UK. It's an easy way to gather all your retirement savings in one place.

Consolidating your pensions is another smart move. Most of us have switched jobs multiple times, leaving behind pension pots each time. You still own those savings, and many personal and workplace pensions can be transferred to a new provider.

Before moving, check with your current providers to see if transfers are allowed. Pay attention to any fees that may apply. Crunch the numbers to decide whether it's worth transferring or better to leave the pension where it is. If you have several small pots, consolidating them can save you from paying fees for each one. It's always a good idea to consult a financial adviser—they can help weigh your options and make the decision easier.

WHAT HAPPENS TO YOUR PENSION IF YOU MOVE ABROAD?

Moving abroad doesn't mean losing access to your pension. I recently helped a relative claim theirs after being away from the UK for over 40 years. The good news is, as long as you've contributed to a workplace pension or paid enough National Insurance contributions, you can claim your pension no matter where you live.

Here's what you need to do:

Claim Your UK State Pension from Abroad

1. **Check Your State Pension Age**: Confirm you've reached the UK State Pension age. You can check online on the government website.
2. **Apply Online, By Phone, or By Post**:
    - **Online**: Apply via the UK government website.
    - **By Phone**:
        - From outside the UK: +44 191 218 7777
        - From the UK: 0800 731 7898
    - **By Post**: Download the international claim form from the government website or contact the International Pension Centre for help.
3. **Contact the International Pension Centre**: They can assist with your claim.
    - **Email**: tvp.internationalqueries@dwp.gov.uk
    - **Phone**: +44 191 218 7777
    - **Postal Address**:

- International Pension Centre
- Tyneview Park
- Newcastle upon Tyne
- NE98 1BA
- United Kingdom

4. **Provide Bank Details**: Make sure your bank can receive payments in your chosen currency.

Claim Your Company Pension from Abroad

1. **Contact Your Pension Provider**: Contact your company's pension administrator for guidance on claiming your pension from abroad.
2. **Submit a Claim Form**: You'll likely need to complete a retirement claim form available online or by post.
3. **Provide Proof of Identity**: You may need to submit a copy of your passport and proof of your address abroad.
4. **Provide Bank Details**: Ensure your bank can accept payments in the currency the pension is paid in.
5. **Get Contact Information**: If you don't have your provider's details, use the **Pension Tracing Service**:
   - **Website**: Pension Tracing Service
   - **Phone**: +44 191 215 4491
   - **Email**: contact-pension-tracing@dwp.gov.uk

From my experience, the process can take a while, so be patient. Ensure you have as many relevant documents, especially if you've been out of the UK for a while. Having the dates you worked and any references will help speed up your claim.

To wrap things up, retirement planning is important, but don't worry—it's never too late to start saving for your future. The headlines about needing millions might seem overwhelming, but what really matters is taking steps that work for your situation. Whether you start small or can contribute more, every little bit adds up. Take advantage of pension schemes and investment opportunities to build a secure and comfortable retirement.

CHAPTER SEVENTEEN—CORE LESSONS

- **Start Early**: The sooner you begin saving, the more time your money has to grow.
- **Maximise Workplace Pensions**: Take full advantage of employer contributions and tax relief.
- **Utilise Personal Pensions**: Benefit from tax relief, flexible access options, and protection from creditors.
- **Delay Retirement**: Working longer reduces the years you'll need to draw from your pension.
- **Create Additional Income Streams**: Use your skills to generate passive income through digital products or part-time work.
- **Reduce Expenses**: Simplify your lifestyle to achieve financial freedom sooner.
- **Cultivate Good Financial Habits**: Pay off debts and save regularly.
- **Consider Retiring Abroad**: Countries with a lower living cost can stretch your pension further.
- **Maintain Good Health**: Adopting a healthy lifestyle can ensure you enjoy retirement in good health and reduce future healthcare costs.

Chapter Seventeen—Exercise

Check Your State Pension Estimate: Visit the government website to check your State Pension estimate. Understanding what you may receive from the state will help you plan your additional retirement savings more effectively.

Explore Workplace Pension: If you're employed but not paying into a pension, check if your employer offers a workplace pension scheme. Take advantage of any employer-matching contributions to boost your retirement savings.

Start a Retirement Fund: If you are self-employed, a freelancer, or an employee who has maxed out their workplace pension, explore opening a retirement savings account, such as a personal or self-invested personal pension (SIPP). Set up regular contributions from your income or bank account, even if it's a small amount. Consistency is crucial.

Chapter Eighteen

PROTECTING YOUR FINANCIAL FUTURE

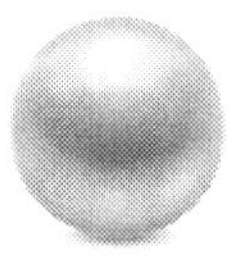

Picture your financial future as a strong fortress, ready to withstand any storm that life throws your way. You've built a solid foundation with budgeting, saving, debt repayment, and investing, but what stands between your hard-earned wealth and potential disaster? That's where protection policies come in—often overlooked but crucial for your financial security.

In this chapter, we'll make sense of insurance and protection covers. It might not be the flashiest topic, but it's essential for keeping your financial fortress strong. We'll look at how the right protection can safeguard your loved ones and your assets from unexpected events. Get ready to clear up common myths and learn how to choose the right protection to keep your financial future secure

PROTECTION POLICIES: OVERCOMING HESITATIONS

Protection policies may not be the most comfortable topic of discussion. The thought of illness or death can stir up feelings of unease, particularly within the African and Black community. Having worked in banking, I've faced challenges in convincing people to consider protection policies that safeguard their loved ones. The reluctance to seek protection doesn't stem from a lack of care for dependents; rather, people hesitate for various reasons:

- Some may worry that obtaining a protection policy shows a lack of faith in divine protection.
- Others fear they somehow invite negative circumstances into their lives by protecting themselves.
- There are even concerns about becoming a target for harm from beneficiaries who stand to benefit from insurance proceeds.
- Many don't trust insurance companies.
- Concerns about affordability.
- Limited knowledge and awareness.
- Fear of exploitation.
- Some hesitate because they fear paying into a policy for years without ever needing to make a claim. But let's pause for a moment—don't we approach other types of insurance in much the same way? We don't bemoan the fact that we haven't needed to claim on our car insurance; instead, we're grateful for the lack of accidents during the covered period. Protection policies operate on a similar principle—they provide peace of mind and financial security, ensuring your loved ones are cared for if the worst happens.

ALIGNING FINANCIAL PROTECTION WITH CULTURAL VALUES AND FAITH

Our African and Black community holds a deep sense of responsibility toward family and loved ones. It is ingrained in the belief that we take care of our own. Protection policies ensure that, even in unforeseen circumstances, your loved ones will be financially secure. It shows you are committed to their well-being, whatever happens.

Does Having Protection Conflict with Faith?

I know of no faith that promises eternal life or constant good health. All faiths teach acceptance of life's uncertainties. Having protection in place means hoping for the best but preparing for the unexpected. It's not declaring faithlessness; it's submitting one's will. I have heard people say, well, if God takes my life, He will look after my family. Well, how can I say this most delicately? That response is called being irresponsible.

Stewardship

Stewardship means taking care of and making good use of what's given to us. By carefully planning and protecting your financial future, you make smart choices to ensure that your hard-earned money lasts and can be passed on to the next generation.

IMPORTANCE OF INSURANCE

Life is a beautiful journey filled with both joyous and challenging moments. We must accept that difficult moments, like illness or death, are also a part of life. I recently had a heartfelt conversation with my daughter about my will. She was understandably uncomfortable with the idea of a time when I wouldn't be here. But as difficult as it may be, facing life's realities is essential.

In 2017, a breast cancer diagnosis shook my world. Naturally, my immediate concern was for my daughters. Amid the uncertainty, I found solace in knowing that they would have some financial security if I were to pass away. While money can never replace a mother, it can ease the burden of financial worries during challenging times.

Insurance coverage is especially important when financial resources are limited. It offers an affordable means to leave assets or money to your family. For instance, by paying a monthly premium, say £20.00, a lump sum running into thousands could be paid out to beneficiaries in the event of a claim.

Imagine a scenario where a family loses its primary breadwinner. The impact and emotional toll are devastating. On top of that, immediate expenses like funeral costs and ongoing living expenses still need to be taken care of. Financial responsibilities don't disappear during difficult times. Proper protection ensures that your loved ones can focus on properly grieving and healing without the added stress of financial burdens.

HOW TO APPROACH PROTECTION POLICIES

Insurance often gets a bad rap. But behind the headlines and horror stories lies a crucial truth: protection policies can be a lifeline in times of uncertainty.

The PPI scandal rocked the nation, leaving millions feeling betrayed and disillusioned. But amid the chaos, there were lessons to be learned. Payment protection insurance—intended to safeguard borrowers against unexpected financial setbacks—was sold recklessly and without consent. Many found themselves saddled with policies that offered little protection when they needed it most.

Like many others, I was bombarded with calls, leaflets, and emails urging me to claim compensation for mis-sold PPI. The outcry was deafening, and the mistrust was palpable. But does this tarnish all insurance policies with the same brush? Absolutely not.

Insurance can greatly enhance financial security if it is understood and used correctly. Understanding, though, is essential. Allow me to use the story of two clients to demonstrate this.

A young, well-off couple came to me to sort out their mortgage. It was a huge mortgage, and both understood the importance of protecting their mortgage and chose comprehensive coverage wisely. I did not need to convince them to take protection cover. They had done their homework and knew what cover they needed. It was the easiest mortgage and protection cover I had ever sold. Little did they know that their decision would soon be put to the test.

About two years later, the wife was diagnosed with cancer. Thanks to their foresight, they could weather that storm. Their protection policy paid off their mortgage in full. Their insurance cover was a much-needed lifeline, easing the burden of mortgage payments during a challenging time.

Contrast the above story with a young man who I also helped with arranging his mortgage. He was tight on money but scraped together a deposit and bought his home. After arranging his home purchase, I explained his insurance coverage options. He was single and opted to buy critical illness coverage but later cancelled the policy after a relative convinced him his coverage was a waste of money. Fate, however, had other plans.

A few months later, tragedy struck. The young man was diagnosed with a debilitating illness, rendering him unable to work. Distraught, he returned to me seeking to reinstate his policy, only to discover it was too late. It is impossible to get coverage for a pre-existing illness. At the time he took out his mortgage, his illness was undiagnosed. Once diagnosed, insurance becomes unattainable. A harsh reality!

What struck me about these stories is that the affluent often understand the value of protection even though they have enough money in other investments to deal with life's surprises. The couple could've paid off their mortgage from their savings and investments without full insurance coverage. But having the cover meant that they didn't have to dip into their savings.

On the other hand, the young man didn't have much saved up. And, he could afford the cover because the premiums were low. If he hadn't cancelled, he'd be enjoying a mortgage-free property and focusing on getting better.

It's like they say, "The rich get richer, and the poor get poorer." I believe the rich often have better information and won't risk losing big money to save a few pennies.

Reflect on these stories. Are you prepared for whatever life throws your way?

To protect your loved ones and your assets, be like the couple described in this story by doing the following:

- **Educate Yourself:** Learn about different insurance types, coverage options, and benefits. This helps you avoid buying unnecessary policies.
- **Choose Reputable Providers:** Research and select insurance companies with solid reputations and good reviews. Recommendations from trusted sources can help.

- **Be Honest:** Always provide accurate information on your application. If unsure about health details, check with your healthcare provider. Accurate info helps avoid future issues.
- **Understand Policy Details:** Read and understand your policy's coverage and exclusions before committing. Clarify any uncertainties with the provider.
- **Consult Experts:** Work with knowledgeable insurance professionals for guidance and personalised advice.
- **Consider Affordability**: Find insurance that fits your budget while providing the coverage you need. Explore various options to balance cost and protection.

Types of Insurance Policy

Let's explore different types of insurance and how they can protect you and your loved ones.

1. **Life Insurance:** Life insurance provides financial security to your beneficiaries in the event of your death by offering a lump sum payment. This payment can cover various expenses such as mortgage repayments, education, or day-to-day living expenses.
2. **Critical Illness Cover:** Critical illness cover provides a one-time lump sum payment if you are diagnosed with a specified critical illness listed in the policy. Common conditions include cancer, heart attacks, strokes, or major organ transplants. This lump sum can manage financial burdens like mortgage repayments, lifestyle adjustments, or other expenses during a critical illness. The beauty of this policy is that even if you fully recover, you keep the money received, providing additional financial security.
3. **Unemployment Insurance:** Unemployment insurance, also known as work insurance, provides financial support if you lose

your job through no fault of your own. It offers monthly payments until you get a new job. However, if you quit or are fired due to your actions, you won't be eligible for this insurance. It's designed for those who were let go because work dried up, or the business closed, or other reasons beyond their control.

4. **Income Protection Insurance:** Income protection insurance ensures a regular income if you cannot work due to illness, injury, or disability. If something stops you from working, like a severe illness or an accident, income protection insurance gives you a portion of your usual earnings. This ongoing payment helps maintain your lifestyle and covers essential financial commitments like mortgage or rent payments, bills, and daily living expenses. Unlike critical illness cover, income protection insurance offers continuous payments until you recover and return to work, reach a specific age, or the policy term ends.
5. **Mortgage Repayment Insurance:** Mortgage repayment insurance helps you cover your mortgage payments if you cannot make them due to illness, injury, or job loss. It ensures that your mortgage repayments continue even when you cannot work and generate income. Typically, this insurance pays out a percentage of your mortgage payment for a specified period, providing relief during challenging times. It's important to carefully review the terms and conditions of the policy to fully understand the coverage provided. A clear understanding ensures that you know what is covered and gives you peace of mind.
6. **Building and Contents Insurance:** Property insurance protects your home from damage or loss caused by fire, theft, or natural disasters. It has two aspects: building insurance, which covers the actual structure of your property, and contents insurance, which protects your personal belongings within the property. Building insurance is often required for homeowners as part of their mortgage conditions, while contents insurance is optional. Both types

of insurance help protect your assets and provide financial security in the event of unexpected incidents.

Reviewing Scenarios:

Let's take a closer look at some real-life situations with our friends Turia, Ayo, Karana, James, and Imani to see how these insurance policies can work in everyday life.

Turia's Protection Considerations: Turia, a lively 20 year old finishing her studies at the University of East London, talks to her bank's adviser about insurance.

Recommendation: The adviser suggests no protection cover for now. Since Turia has no assets, liabilities, or dependents, there would be no financial impact if something happened to her. Her student loan would be wiped out if she died or couldn't work, and she doesn't need building or content insurance while living with her parents.

Turia's Decision: After she starts working, Turia plans to look into life and critical illness insurance and start saving to build an emergency fund.

—

Ayo's Protection Considerations: Ayo is also single but with a demanding job and a mortgage. His adviser doesn't recommend life insurance as he too has no dependents who would be financially affected if he passed away. The bank would sell the property to recover their loan, with any excess going to Ayo's estate.

Recommendation: The adviser recommends critical illness cover, which would provide a lump sum if Ayo is diagnosed with a severe illness, helping with mortgage payments, medical expenses, or lifestyle adjustments.

Income protection, unemployment, and mortgage repayment insurance are also suggested to cover financial support if Ayo cannot work.

Ayo's Decision: Despite the adviser's recommendation against life insurance, Ayo decides to take out a policy. He wants to ensure his property passes to his family, not to lenders if he were to pass away. With life cover, his mortgage will be paid off, and the property will go to those he names in his will. Ayo also takes out critical illness and content insurance for his flat. He opts out of income protection and unemployment insurance due to high premiums, relying instead on his fully-funded emergency fund. Ayo plans to explore passive income sources for additional income as a long-term financial strategy.

—

Karana's Protection Considerations: Karana, a single mother with seven-year-old twins, is surprised when her adviser recommends life and critical illness insurance. She initially thought insurance was only for the wealthy. However, the adviser explains that insurance is crucial to protect her children's future, especially when resources are limited. While wealthier individuals may have the means to handle life's challenges, insurance provides essential protection for those with fewer resources.

Recommendation: The adviser suggests life and critical illness insurance to ensure financial support for her sons. Karana can also use a will, appoint a legal guardian, and set up trusts to manage the insurance funds for her children if she is no longer around.

Karana's Decision: Karana chooses life and critical illness insurance with £100,000 coverage for 14 years until her twins turn 21. Although she would like unemployment and income protection insurance, it is unaffordable, and her work contract type makes her ineligible. She is now committed to building an emergency fund to prepare for the unexpected.

Imani and James's Protection Considerations: Meet Imani and James, a power couple navigating the world of finance and family. Imani is the CEO of a major investment bank, while James is a dedicated stay-at-home dad to their little ones, Remi and Jonah.

Their adviser highlights the need for comprehensive protection insurance, including joint life and critical illness coverage for both Imani and James. At first, James is confused. He doesn't contribute financially to the mortgage and wonders why he needs this insurance.

Recommendation: The adviser explains that protecting both partners is essential. If something were to happen to James, it would deeply impact their family. Although losing Imani's income would be tough, losing James means Imani might have to juggle work with full-time childcare. This protection would help cover the mortgage if an unforeseen event occurs, giving Imani the financial flexibility to focus on her family or plan her next steps without added stress.

Imani and James's Decision: Imani and James decide to take out life and critical illness cover for both of them. This ensures their mortgage will be paid off if either of them faces a severe illness or passes away. They also opt for income protection and unemployment coverage to safeguard against job loss. Building and contents insurance will protect their home and belongings.

In conclusion, whether you're starting out in life like Turia, juggling responsibilities like Ayo, securing your family's future like Karana, or managing a household with a partner like Imani and James, protection insurance is important. It goes beyond just covering your bases—it's about feeling secure and prepared for whatever life throws your way. Take the time to understand your needs and explore your options. Give yourself and your loved ones the gift of peace. Adequate coverage is an investment in your future well-being and stability. Planning ahead today can make all the difference tomorrow.

CHAPTER EIGHTEEN—CORE LESSONS

- Protecting your loved ones and assets through insurance is vital to financial planning.
- Budgeting, saving, and investing are essential, but all your hard work could be at risk without adequate protection.
- Insurance policies, such as life insurance, critical illness cover, unemployment cover, and income protection, provide financial security against unexpected events.
- Proper protection ensures that your loved ones are financially supported if you pass away or fall critically ill.
- Protection is for everybody, regardless of wealth or financial resources.
- The fewer financial resources you have, the greater your need for protection.
- Not having protection can perpetuate poverty from one generation to the next.
- By prioritising protection, you break the cycle of financial vulnerability and create a secure future for yourself and your loved ones.
- It safeguards your assets and helps maintain the standard of living for your family.

Chapter Eighteen—Exercise

Assess your current insurance coverage: Review your existing insurance policies and determine if they adequately protect your loved ones and assets. Consider factors like life insurance, critical illness coverage, and income protection.

PASSING THE TORCH

Now that you have the tools to build wealth and take control of your financial future, it's time to share your newfound wisdom and guide other Black women on their journey.

By leaving your honest review on Amazon, you'll help other Black women discover the same empowerment you've gained. Your review can light the way for those seeking financial freedom and inspire them to take that first step.

I appreciate your support. Wealth-building thrives when we share our knowledge, and you're helping me do just that.

Scan the QR Code below to leave your review on Amazon.

With gratitude,

Joyce

Closing Reflections

Congratulations! You've completed a transformative journey through this book, tackling the essential aspects of personal finance tailored to the unique challenges faced by Black women. Each chapter has been a stepping stone toward empowerment, helping you understand our financial landscape, embrace resilience, and take charge of your financial destiny.

We've confronted the often-unspoken challenges we face and how our backgrounds shape our views on money. From the "Black tax" to the intersections of race and gender with finance, we've explored practical strategies for becoming savvy money managers.

This book aims to show you that you are not alone in your financial journey. Thousands of Black women are walking this path with you. Even "skilled" professionals like me have faced financial struggles, so there's no guilt or shame in where you are now. **Fixing our finances has no age limit, and it's never too late to take control.**

Starting any self-development journey can feel overwhelming, but simply picking up this book and reading it through is a significant accomplishment. You're already winning, so take a deep breath and approach your financial goals one step at a time.

Now that you've reached the end, what should you do next? *Here are some practical steps:*

1. **Reflect:** Consider how your childhood and cultural background influence your financial habits and beliefs.
2. **Take Stock:** Assess your current financial situation—your income, expenses, assets, and debts.
3. **Set SMART Goals:** Define specific, measurable, achievable, relevant, and time-bound financial objectives.
4. **Apply Your Learning:** Create a budget, track your spending, and build your emergency fund.
5. **Stay Committed:** Stay motivated and adaptable as you work towards your goals. **Change takes time, so be patient with yourself.**

You should now understand that mastering personal finance isn't an impossible challenge—it's entirely within your reach. The exercises at the end of each chapter are keys to unlocking your financial potential. Building new habits takes time, so revisit these exercises as often as needed and let them guide you toward your financial dreams.

Sorting out your finances is just the beginning. **Your responsibility extends to your family, descendants, and community.** This book aims to spark a broader transformation within the Black community.

Actual change takes time and intention. The Office for National Statistics (ONS) shows that the UK Asian community, particularly Indians, is wealthier on average, primarily due to sharing financial knowledge across generations**. This should inspire us.** We can build wealth, too, by teaching our children about money as a wealth-building tool and making wise choices from an early age. They can ensure the next generation has a solid platform to build on and improve upon.

Financial literacy should be an everyday conversation in our households. The ONS data shows that much of our wealth is tied up in assets that lose value over time. **Let's shift our focus to building lasting**

wealth—investments, savings, and assets that grow and secure our future.

No matter your age**, it's never too late to start** building wealth. Wealth-building is a generational effort, with each generation contributing.

Connect with me on my website, www.simplemoneyhacks.com. Your feedback is gold; it will shape future editions of this book and ensure I serve you better.

As you close this book**, use the knowledge you've gained to empower yourself and uplift your community.** Together, we can leave financial illiteracy behind.

Remember, this isn't the end of your journey—it's just the beginning. Every step you take brings you closer to financial freedom. **Believe in yourself, take action, and watch your financial dreams become reality.**

Thank you for allowing me to be your guide on this journey. Your commitment to your future is truly commendable.

Warm regards,
Joyce

Acknowledgments

I am deeply grateful to my daughters, Mayowa and Eniola. Your unwavering belief in me has been the foundation of my strength through every twist and turn of this journey. Your love, encouragement, and constant support have been unmatched. Thank you for being my sounding board, helping with research, and offering feedback that always pushes me to do better. I am blessed beyond measure to have you both by my side.

To my dad, the kindest and most generous soul I've ever known—your love, even in your absence, continues to guide and inspire me. I miss you every day, but I feel your presence in all that I do. Your influence on my life is immeasurable, and I will forever be grateful for the time we had together. You are not forgotten; you live on in my heart and in everything I achieve.

To my sister, Sade—your memory is a constant source of strength. Though you're no longer with me, your spirit remains close, reminding me of the unconditional love and acceptance that only you could give. I carry that with me always, and it fuels my determination to keep moving forward.

A heartfelt thank you to my dear friend Ibi. You kept me grounded when everything seemed overwhelming, and your support has been invaluable. Thank you for always being there. Your wisdom, and steady presence keep me grounded.

I also want to express my deep appreciation to my editor, Dana. Your expertise, patience, and meticulous attention to detail transformed my words into something far better than I could have done alone. Thank you for being such a crucial part of this journey.

My gratitude extends to every student I've had the privilege to mentor. Your journeys, insights, and successes have enriched this book beyond measure. A special shout-out to Maria G., Demelza, Carina, Dorcas, Doctor Kris (you know who you are), and Helen K. Your financial victories inspire me to keep sharing my knowledge. Each of you has left a lasting impact on me, and I am honoured to have been part of your journey, which will continue to influence my work in the future.

Finally, to all the students whose paths I've crossed—you are my greatest teachers. Your unique perspectives and experiences have enriched my understanding of financial education. Thank you for trusting me with your financial education. It has been a privilege to walk alongside you.

References

Advertising Association/WARC Expenditure Report. (2024, July 29). *UK advertising spend reached £9.2BN in Q1 2024.* https://www.warc.com/expenditurereport

AHAIC Commission Members. (2025, March 05). Executive summary: *The state of universal health coverage in Africa.* AHAIC. https://ahaic.org/download/executive-summary-the-state-of-universal-health-coverage-in-africa/

Anti-Money Laundering. (2024, June 11). *Bank and church money laundering: Ecclesiastical crime.* FCA: Financial Crime Academy. https://financialcrimeacademy.org/bank-and-church-money-laundering-ecclesiastical-crime/

Business Insider. (2024, January 22*). I retired and moved to Thailand. It's cheap, and I feel more respected here than in the UK.* https://www.businessinsider.com/retired-abroad-thailand-cheaper-respectful-retiree-resort-2024-1

Cocheo, S. (2024). 2024 marketing roadmap: *More customer focus, more streamlining & fresh takes on life's milestones.* The Financial Brand. https://thefinancialbrand.com/news/bank-marketing/2024-bank-marketing-trends-demand-more-spending-171736

Cox, Josie. (2023, March 1). *The problem confronting women of colour.* BBC. https://www.bbc.com/worklife/article/20230228-the-perfect-storm-keeping-women-of-colour-behind-at-work

Dyomfana, Z. (2022, April 28). *Black tax—burden or investment?* Investec. https://www.investec.com/en_za/focus/investing/black-tax.html

England and Wales census 2021 - rm031: *Ethnic group by religion - UK Data Service.* (n.d.). UK Data Service. https://statistics.ukdataservice.ac.uk/dataset/england-and-wales-census-2021-rm031-ethnic-group-by-religion

Global Citizen Solutions. (2024). *The cost of living in Spain 2024: The complete guide for expats.* https://www.globalcitizensolutions/spain-cost-of-living/

Gov.UK Ethnicity Facts and Figures. (2021, March 4). *Renting social housing.* https://www.ethnicity-facts-figures.service.gov.uk/housing/social-housing/renting-from-a-local-authority-or-housing-association-social-housing/latest/

Halifax. (2023, March 15). *Homeowners are nearly £500 better off annually than renters.* Lloyds Banking Group. https://www.lloydsbankinggroup.com/media/press-releases/2023/halifax-2023/homeowners-nearly-500-better-off-than-renters.html#:~:text=Homeowners%20there%20now%20pay%20%C2%A3,off%20than%20renters%20each%20year

Hamel, K., Tong, B., & Hofer, M. (n.d.). *Poverty in Africa is now falling—But not fast enough.* Brookings. https://www.brookings.edu/articles/poverty-in-africa-is-now-falling-but-not-fast-enough/

International Labour Organization. (2014, September 30). Sub-Saharan Africa: *Only one in five older persons receives old-age pension.* International Labour Organization. https://www.ilo.org/resource/news/sub-saharan-africa-only-one-five-older-persons-receives-old-age-pension

International Living. (2023, January 13). *Retiring in Malaysia - Malaysia just might be the place for you.* https://internationalliving.com/countries/malaysia/retire-in-malaysia/

Joseph Rowntree Foundation. (n.d.). *How do we defuse the pensioner poverty time bomb?* https://www.jrf.org.uk/savings-debt-and-assets/how-do-we-defuse-the-pensioner-poverty-time-bomb

Kelch-Oliver, K., & Ancis, J. R. (2011). *Black women's body image: An analysis of culture-specific influences.* Women & Therapy, 34(4), 345–358. https://doi.org/10.1080/02703149.2011.592065

London School of Economics and Political Science. (2021, March 3). *Black women are least likely to be among UK's top earners.* https://www.lse.ac.uk/News/Latest-news-from-LSE/2021/c-March-21/Black-women-are-least-likely-to-be-among-UKs-top-earners

Maverick, J. B. (2024, January 3). *What is the average annual return of the S&P 500?* Investopedia. https://www.investopedia.com/ask/answers/042415/what-average-annual-return-sp-500.asp

Office for National Statistics. (2020, November 23). *Household wealth by ethnicity, Great Britain: April 2016 to March 2018.* https://www.ons.gov.uk/peoplepopulationandcommunity/personalandhouseholdfinances/incomeandwealth/articles/householdwealthbyethnicitygreatbritain/april2016tomarch2018

Office for National Statistics. (2021, July 26). *Ethnic differences in life expectancy and mortality from selected causes in England and Wales: 2011 to 2014.* https://www.ons.gov.uk/peoplepopulationandcommunity/birthsdeathsandmarriages/lifeexpectancies/articles/ethnicdifferencesinlifeexpectancyandmortalityfromselectedcausesinenglandandwales/2011to2014

Office for National Statistics. (2023, May 10). *Families in England and Wales:* Census 2021. Office for National Statistics. https://www.ons.gov.uk/peoplepopulationandcommunity/birthsdeathsandmarriages/families/articles/familiesinenglandandwales/census2021

Ramsey. (2021, September 27). *Money, marriage, and communication.* Ramsey Solutions. https://www.ramseysolutions.com/relationships/money-marriage-communication-research

Retirement Living Standards. (n.d.). *Understanding retirement living standards.* https://www.retirementlivingstandards.org.uk/

Retire in the Caribbean. (n.d.). *Retire in Jamaica.* https://www.retireinthecaribbean.com/countries/retire-in-jamaica/

Scottish Widows. (2021). *Overworked and underprepared: Black women face retirement challenges.* Scottish Widows. https://www.scottishwidows.co.uk/about-us/media-centre/press-releases/overworked-and-underprepared.html

Sethi, R. (2009). *I Will Teach You To Be Rich.* Hodder & Stoughton. Published in the UK, 2010.

Siegel, C. (2016). *Why didn't they teach me this in school? 99 personal money management principles to live by* (Narrated by D. Sluyter) [Audiobook]. Simple Strategic LLC. Audible.

UK Government. (n.d.). Student loan cancellation. https://www.gov.uk/guidance/student-loan-cancellation-if-a-customer-dies and https://www.gov.uk/guidance/student-loan-cancellation-permanently-unfit-to-work

Unbiased. (2023, December 11). *What happens to my pension if I move abroad?* https://www.unbiased.co.uk/discover/pensions-retirement/planning-for-retirement/retiring-abroad

UNESCO. (n.d.). *Education in Africa.* https://uis.unesco.org/en/topic/education-africa

Vaters, K. (n.d.). *The invisible scandal: How bad debt and poor stewardship are killing the church's reputation.* Pivot | A Blog by Karl Vaters. https://

www.christianitytoday.com/karl-vaters/2018/august/invisible-scandal-bad-debt-poor-stewardship-killing-church.html

WOB Directors. (n.d.). *Hidden truth: Diversity on boards in UK listed firms.* WOB: Women on Boards. https://wbdirectors.co.uk/

Made in the USA
Columbia, SC
11 July 2025